CW00732735

The Half of It

The Half of It

A Memoir

Madison Beer

HARPER

An Imprint of HarperCollins*Publishers*

THE HALF OF IT. Copyright © 2023 by Madison Beer. All rights reserved. Printed in the United States of America. No part of this book may be used or reproduced in any manner whatsoever without written permission except in the case of brief quotations embodied in critical articles and reviews. For information, address HarperCollins Publishers, 195 Broadway, New York, NY 10007.

HarperCollins books may be purchased for educational, business, or sales promotional use. For information, please email the Special Markets Department at SPsales@harpercollins.com.

FIRST EDITION

Designed by Kyle O'Brien

Library of Congress Cataloging-in-Publication Data has been applied for.

ISBN 978-0-06-323769-8

23 24 25 26 27 LBC 5 4 3 2 1

For my mother, my brother, and my father—
thank you. I know it hasn't been easy.

For the younger Madison I'm writing this
about—thank you for getting me here.

I hope I've made you proud.

Contents

Preface

It's 9:53 on a Wednesday night. I just finished writing the final chapter of this book in my bathtub, and now I find myself here—back at the beginning, meeting you. Before we jump into the thick of it all, I want to take a moment and let you know why I wrote this book in the first place—how we got here.

I'm unsure why I was given the privileged life that I have, when there are millions of girls just like me across the globe who will never be afforded the same opportunities. I wanted to approach this book as carefully as possible, with the understanding of my inherently privileged position. My story is one in a sea of many more vibrant, important narratives, and my day-to-day worries are much different from most, but I only ever wanted to write a book to remind you that someone who might appear more than fine on the outside still has her own share of demons and battles she wasn't sure she would make it out alive from.

Truthfully, writing this has opened some unhealed wounds. I talk about a lot of things I hadn't planned on talking about. I realized I was sugarcoating a lot of things—not only to myself but to the people who have been listening all this time. I made connections between events in my early years and emotional instability issues I still struggle with to this day.

I'm the most openly honest I've ever been in the following pages, but that isn't to say I talk about everything I've been through in this book. No matter how much you think you know me, there will always be parts of my story that are for me and me only. That's kind of the point—you never know everything, even when you think you might. You never know the silent battles people are fighting, even the people you think you're closest to. You'll never walk in my shoes, and I'll never walk in yours. And we shouldn't have to in order to empathize with each other.

I want my story to represent more than just me. While it's a story of my life, it's also a story about the power of empathy and understanding, and what something as simple as human kindness can do in changing someone's life. If I can do any good by sharing my own personal experiences, I'll never hesitate to speak up.

With that being said, just because it happened this way, that doesn't mean it should have.

The Half of It

1

The Half of It

Music surrounds all of my earliest memories. I listened to all genres from an early age. Like most kids, I was always drawn to creating things and sharing them with people. My dad was decent on the guitar, and every night I begged him to strum me a new song I could sing along to. Whenever we had company, I'd demand their attention and put on a show for them. And even once I burned them out, I'd hide away in my bedroom and write my own music. Very early on, it became my way to escape.

I think that's how it starts for most children—dancing, singing, and performing are all so self-expressive that we're drawn to them instinctually, like they're part of our human nature. I wasn't swayed by the idea of flashing lights and big crowds. As a young girl I adored the Cheetah Girls, but I wanted to be like them because they got to dance and sing on a stage and connect with people through their music, not because they were famous. I would have wanted to perform whether ten people were watching me or ten thousand. I was just happy to be singing.

From the time I was a child watching Disney Channel all the way up to when I first moved to LA, my idea of what being a "celebrity" entailed was romanticized and distorted, because I was watching from the outside. I didn't understand that, as a viewer, I was being shown carefully curated moments that the actors and their networks wanted me to see. Young, impressionable kids see a five-minute clip and think it's representative of a person's entire life. It takes a while to realize how much is really going on behind the scenes. And who is really to blame? Those who take part in the system built around them, or the people who built the system in the first place?

When I was first signed and started working in the industry— once I got to experience a taste of it for myself—it came as a huge culture shock. I went through a big learning curve as I tried to figure out what was real and what was fake. And I struggled to separate the fantasy I created in my head from the reality of what it *actually* takes to make a career work.

Before I was signed, I imagined it like this—I would move to LA and be caught up in a whirlwind of music and performances. I'd meet a group of girls in similar positions, and we'd all become best friends. People in the industry would be welcoming and excited to work with me, because I was young and talented and they'd want to guide me in the right direction. For a while, that's what it felt like. But the truth revealed itself to me with time.

Instead, I went to parties and watched people who hated each other pose and giggle for a video together and then go back to sitting on their phones in silence. I tagged along to friends' video shoots and saw how they only smiled when the cameras came into the room to film behind-the-scenes footage. I sat in meetings and had every one of my ideas shot down because I was too young or too inexperienced, which was a fair point and a valid reason—but it isn't what I thought I was signing up for. In a lot of ways, I felt like I'd been lied to.

When I talk about my experience, I am aware that I have to tread lightly. A lot of celebrities and people in any sort of limelight receive backlash for talking about the negative side of fame, for "complaining" about being in such an undoubtedly privileged position. Of course I understand why. We see celebrities as people who have everything. Things like losing all privacy, or being constantly up for criticism—even on things that don't pertain to the job—are just deemed "part of it."

It's almost like an unspoken rule. You can't complain because you've been given such an incredible opportunity. It's true. But there's a balance. I have more overwhelming support and love than the average person, this I can acknowledge. I can sing a song I wrote in tears in my room to a crowd of people who love and care, how special is that? Luckily over the years I've been able to check myself and try to say, "Hey, this is one negative comment in a sea of positive ones, choose to respond to the love instead." But at twelve, it wasn't so easy.

If you make a mean comment about a friend at school, you're a bully who will most likely face consequences. But if you make a mean comment about someone online, no one bats an eye. That simple switch is frightening to me. What changed? Why should your words hurt less? Why would they *not* affect someone? People seem to think that because the benefits of fame are so high, the downsides are automatically overshadowed. The fact that I was an insecure child just trying to navigate a very new and intimidating world was always overlooked. Any type of sympathy was always lacking.

I don't want to glorify the position I'm in by boasting about all the upsides. Glazing over the downsides of being so publicly visible only does everyone a disservice, and keeps us in a self-feeding cycle that places fame at the top of some societal hierarchy. If I only talk about the good things, I'm sending the message to my young fans that I have a perfect life, that this career path is something to idolize.

But there are upsides and downsides to everything. When my parents, grandparents, and only sibling are receiving death threats on social media just because they're related to me, it's a big downside. When the police show up at my house in the middle of the night because someone's made a threat against my life, it's a downside. There are certain violations of human boundaries that I find inexcusable, no matter the position I'm in.

So even though my career is responsible for all of my proudest, happiest moments, it's also been to blame for some of my lowest. This is why I can't help feeling that if I don't speak openly about my struggles as a result of fame, I would be complicit in selling a false narrative. I have a lot of young fans who look up to me. The last thing I want is for them to see my life and think it's an end goal. Social media does that enough already, and I don't feel like reducing something so serious to a teary-eyed Instagram photo is fair to anyone, let alone myself. I'm talking to you here because by picking up this book and choosing to read it, you have made the choice to meet me halfway. I'm happy you have.

In the decade I've been working, the entire climate of social media has changed completely. Fame and online virality have only become more and more attainable as new social platforms continue to appear. I went through it over ten years ago, before apps like TikTok even existed, before the term *influencer* was coined. Back then, it took a viral tweet from one of the biggest pop stars in the world to get my name out there, but today someone can post a fifteen-second TikTok and go viral overnight. And just like that, they have a shot at a career. "Fame" is more accessible now than ever. While this isn't always a bad thing, I think it's important to proceed with caution.

Now, studies show that "social media influencer" and "YouTuber" are two of the top careers that eleven-to-sixteen-year-olds aspire to.[*] On one hand, I think it's amazing that so many kids are interested in a field full of creativity and self-expression, but I also worry that so many of us are drawn to these platforms for all the wrong reasons—that the propaganda "dream job" they think they want is nothing like it seems.

Don't get me wrong, the internet is a great tool for someone who wants to make videos about something they're passionate about, or connect with other people who have the same interests. But I experience firsthand how the emphasis on celebrities in this

---

[*] Paul Skeldon, "Young Affiliates: Nearly a Fifth of British Children Aspire to Be Social Media Influencers: Marketing & Promotion," Telemedia Online, February 14, 2022, https://www.telemediaonline.co.uk/young-affiliates-nearly-a-fifth-of-british-children-aspire-to-be-social-media-influencers/.

generation is teaching kids that in order to be valid, they have to be *seen*.

There are a lot of talented people who will never pursue fame. Some people go viral overnight and then disappear because the negativity online was too overwhelming. There are a lot of people who are given the same exact opportunity as me and choose not to take it.

And it's not because they weren't talented enough, not because they didn't work hard enough, not because they didn't *want* it badly enough. It's because they got a glimpse behind the curtain and decided it wasn't for them. When a celebrity slowly steps back from the spotlight, or an artist stops making music, it doesn't mean they're a failure. It usually means they've made a decision not to equate their art with a world that is hyperfocused on numbers and perceived means of success.

Here's the thing: fame is merely a side effect of the career I've chosen. It's not the reward or the end goal.

From the start, I only ever wanted to make music—to write and sing lyrics that meant something to me. I've only ever wanted to create.

If my goals were different—if I had only used singing as an avenue to gain followers, to get likes on photos, or to become rich and famous—I wouldn't have stuck it out for this long. And I would be miserable. There's no genuine fulfillment in something that vapid, at least not for me. All my peers who entered the industry chasing fame and money have burned out just as quickly as they've started. And the crash afterward isn't pretty.

A lot of people write stories about their life when they feel they've come to a good closing point. I've finished a few chapters of my life, but I'm still in the middle of my story.

Instead, I want my story and all of its specificity to speak to something bigger. This isn't me whining and saying, "I went through so much, life is hard!" There are so many upsides to what I do. But most people already know them. Instead, this is me saying, "Because I went through this, I have this insight to share with you." I believe what I've been through speaks to some of the larger issues plaguing my generation.

Mostly, I want to be honest. Even if some people receive it the wrong way, I'd rather make that sacrifice if it means my audience views me on a human level.

I want to demystify what someone in my position goes through—which isn't all that different from the issues most young adults deal with. I just have more eyes on me. There's nothing different in my DNA that makes me immune to hate or suffering just because I've been incredibly fortunate in my career. I'm sharing my story in hopes that it might make some of you feel less alone. I just ask that you please be gentle with me as I open up about some of the more difficult things I've been through.

It took me a long time to develop the mindset I have now, though, so before we spend too much time in the present, we have to go back to where my journey started.

2

Smoke and Mirrors

I spent so much of my childhood surrounded by music. I tried my hand at several different hobbies—gymnastics, karate, swimming—but singing was always the thing that came naturally to me. It was my constant.

I was a natural-born performer. Both of my parents encouraged me, but as I got older and I continued to stick with it, I realized it was a part of me the same way breathing was. I wasn't just a little girl who sang because she liked the sound of her own voice, I had a budding talent and the passion to back it up.

My dad got me into a few modeling gigs when I was younger, and they were easy enough, but singing was the thing that stuck with me. I practiced constantly on my own. My daily routine included locking myself in my room and trying to hit all of Miley Cyrus's high notes in "The Climb" until my ears were ringing. After school, I stayed behind to participate in a club called School of Rock, only to go home and practice the songs we'd learned well past dinner.

But for the most part I was a normal kid. I loved performing, but I was well aware that I was one of millions who felt the same, that it wasn't anything out of the ordinary. And it wasn't something attainable. I knew Justin Bieber's story—how he was discovered and signed and quickly skyrocketed—but that was a one-in-a-billion chance.

When I got a little older, I became obsessed with YouTube and particularly obsessed with cover artists like Christina Grimmie. But that was about as far as my dreams went—I thought *maybe*, one day, if I was good enough, I could post my own covers online. At the time that was the extent of my dream. The thought of turning singing into a full-time career never felt realistic.

But my life was still saturated with music. Both my parents believed in me, and my dad really gave me that extra push I needed. His aspirations for me felt so outlandish and exaggerated that I would always laugh it off when he bragged to his friends, saying how it was only a matter of time before his daughter would sell out Madison Square Garden.

But however far-fetched, his praise boosted my confidence, and when I was twelve years old, my mom's friend invited us to his small studio space in New York on an off day, just so I could play around in a real booth and get a feel for what recording music was actually like.

I agreed instantly. To be able to go to a *real-life* studio? Where *real-life* singers have performed? It was unimaginable for a preteen girl. I was flooded with ideas. I stayed up late trying to pick which songs I wanted to cover, and putting together different arrangements and mash-ups that I wanted to try.

To put into perspective just how young I was, I got my braces off the same week I recorded my first cover. My parents and I posted the cover on YouTube, mainly just so my mom could share it on Facebook for our close family and friends to see. I wanted people in our town to know that I sang, but that was the extent of it. YouTube was still fairly new, and "influencers" didn't exist yet. I was in a math support class when my video hit a hundred views, and that was a shock within itself. Anything more was unimaginable.

The following months were quite the whirlwind, to say the least. I was pulled out of school in the middle of my seventh-grade year after being signed by one of the biggest managers and pop stars in the business. I couldn't believe what was happening.

I went from being a completely normal kid in Long Island to practically living on an airplane overnight. I was living a double life between New York and Los Angeles—a city I had only seen in my dreams.

Starting my career so young was intense, to put it mildly, from being in the studio until two o'clock in the morning to taking meetings at some of the biggest television networks and balancing homeschool tutoring and homework on top of that. Sometimes I forget how young I was when I made such big life decisions—ones I wasn't even sure I was qualified to make at twelve years old.

My greatest aspirations had come true. I'd landed a one-in-a-billion shot at a dream life, and the world stretched out before my fingertips. To me, LA was the Hollywood from movies and TV shows. It was where I needed to be.

My short trips to California were spent being whisked

around, given a taste of everything I could have if I moved there full-time. I was taken backstage at *The Voice*, Wango Tango, and iHeartRadio events, introduced to every celebrity I looked up to as a kid, and connected with big names behind the scenes. I got to go to London, where Justin Bieber brought me onstage at the O2 arena and sang "Happy Birthday" to me in front of twenty thousand people. (Talk about a happy fourteenth birthday.) Everything moved so fast, and it was all so surreal. It felt like I was watching a movie of my life instead of actually living it for myself.

I was young enough that it was smart to keep the darker side of the industry hidden from me, but this meant that it was easier for me to fall in love with the lifestyle when all I was exposed to were the shiny, instantly gratifying positives. I spent my trips to LA on overdrive, bright-eyed and bushy-tailed, and then I'd fly back home and sit in my living room in New York and feel like I didn't know what to do with myself. It always took a few days for me to adjust to being back home again, to decompress from the constant excitement running through my veins.

I loved my home in New York. I was always an involved student, in and out of class, and I had a huge friend group made up of girls I'd known since I was in diapers. But once I was pulled out of school—once I started splitting my time between coasts—I became more and more isolated at home. During the day all my friends were in class at the middle school we once shared, and I was being homeschooled in my bedroom. I spent all year counting down the days until I could go back to my favorite summer camp, only to be devastated when I was told I couldn't go. Two months off so I could be at sleepaway camp wasn't realistic—I had work to do. This is something I still grieve to this day.

I started to feel like an outsider. My friends were drifting away, and I felt like we had nothing in common anymore. Being alienated at home only meant I drew more and more to Los Angeles, to the fast-paced world that kept me distracted—the constant stimulation that kept me from thinking about all my best friends at home growing up without me.

I didn't see the man behind the curtain for a few years, but as I visited LA more and more often, I started having my own experiences working in the industry. As the novelty began to wear off, I was left with an odd feeling in my stomach that took me a few more years to fully pin down—if I wasn't careful, I would lose myself to this.

3

The Man Behind the Curtain

Being signed was my dream come true, but I had a lot less control than I thought I would.

That was my first rude awakening when my career really got into motion. I was newly thirteen, but I didn't understand how young I actually was—how I would be viewed walking into meetings with my team and pitching all of my outlandish ideas. I'd built it up in my head. I imagined they'd sit me down and ask me about the kind of career I wanted, what kind of songs I wanted to sing, and we'd work together on building a plan from there.

Instead, it was like I was given a mold and told to squeeze myself into it. Before I'd even gotten on the plane and set foot in Los Angeles, a lot of people already had an idea of what they wanted me to be. I expected to be taken a lot more seriously, but I was so young that my ability to give my own creative input was overlooked. Instead of letting me find an image and a sound organically, they'd already created the brand around my name. Madison

Beer was a character, and I was just a girl reading the script they'd already written for me.

"We have big plans for you," I heard over and over from everyone around me. Albums, acting gigs, reality shows . . . they were all rolled out in front of me like a red carpet. And because I was so young—because I hadn't had any experiences that taught me otherwise—I believed it all. I trusted the people who said they had my best interests at heart. I hung on every word they said, every lofty promise they made, and because I got my hopes up so high, it was even more devastating when those promises got broken.

In writing about those years, I see things differently now. My perspective has changed a lot and it continues to. I don't feel resentful or upset about everything not panning out exactly how it was pitched to me or how we thought it would. It was no one's fault, really. But despite all my acceptance and hesitancy to point fingers, I still wish that the adults responsible for me had taken more time to consider the potential consequences these experiences could have on me in the long run. I think we all got carried away.

Truthfully, I never really cared for the first song I released. From the moment I first heard it until it came out, it just didn't feel right. There was nothing wrong with the song, but it never felt like *me*. I didn't connect with it, even at thirteen. It wasn't how I wanted to introduce myself to the world.

I assumed the direction I would continue in would mirror the videos that got me signed in the first place—singing passionate songs I felt connected to. My voice lent itself to ballads, and I was always more drawn to soulful music with real lyrics, to songs that dripped with emotion. A song was only a good song if I could close my eyes and picture it as the backing track of a pivotal movie scene. Even if I hadn't gone through heartbreak at thirteen years old, I still wanted to sing about it. I was comparing myself to fully established adult singers, not to other kids my age. I had high hopes and big dreams.

But, understandably, there wasn't demand for a preteen who wanted to sing ballads. Because of my age, I was automatically branded to a certain audience. It was the most logical move to throw me in with the Disney and Nickelodeon kids, to stick to the safety of bubblegum pop. I was a cute teenage girl with a decent singing voice—it only made sense. It was what worked, and I understood that. So even if it wasn't my first choice, at the end of the day, I was just excited to be making music, no matter the form.

Three days before the music video shoot, I had my first fitting. That was the first time I was directly confronted with the role I was being asked to step into. The outfits that were chosen for me were full of crazy colors, purposely mismatched patterns, and girly designs that looked nothing like what was in my actual closet at home. I frowned at myself in the floor-length mirror and spoke up tentatively.

"This doesn't feel like me," I said, finding my mom's eyes in the reflection. I turned to her, picking at the skirt I had on. "It just feels too . . . cutesy. Could we switch it with jeans or something?"

"I think it's cute." My mom looked at me, nodding toward the stylist, who was still in the room.

I nodded to myself, turning back to the mirror and plastering a smile on my face, trying to make it work. I didn't feel like *me*, but I managed. I knew it was just part of the game I needed to play to get ahead. It was the same path everyone else before me had followed—so I figured I could make it work, even if it felt slightly off. I pushed that thought aside.

It wasn't until we were in the car that I broke down in tears.

"What, Madison?" My mom was completely caught off guard. "What is it?"

I didn't know what to tell her. I didn't know why I felt so wrong. And I was upset with myself for being so unhappy on a day that was supposed to be so new and celebratory.

"It just feels weird," I admitted. "It feels cheesy."

"They know what they're doing," she tried to assure me. "Just look at it like you're playing a character. You have fun doing that. I want you to be happy, but we should try and give them a chance first."

I took a deep breath and looked at myself in the side mirror of the car, feeling stupid for crying. I rubbed my eyes raw on the back of my sleeve and spent the rest of the ride home in silence.

This world was just as new to my parents as it was to me, and none of us really had any idea what we were doing. I think their caution stemmed from not wanting to step on anyone's toes, and none of us knew where to draw the line between having an opinion and being ungrateful. I felt like anything I said that *might* offend the higher-ups would result in the worst-case scenario. One wrong move, one wrong word, and I'd be stripped of everything and tossed on a flight back home. Everything was stemming from a place of wanting to support me and my dreams. I don't think my parents were trying to silence or scare me out of voicing an opinion, but at times they did.

This was one of those moments. I had to suck it up, biting the bullet and wearing the very outfit that had me in tears in the music video, because god forbid I do anything to poke the bear. I kept quiet, just to avoid the argument and keep myself from being seen as ungrateful.

In the moment, I never could have foreseen the snowball effect it would have. It seemed like a small sacrifice in the grand scheme of things. Pay the small price of wearing an ugly outfit to be able to star in your own music video? No-brainer. But looking back, it had deeper roots. This was the first time (but far from the last) that I was taught how to do something that I still spend so much time trying to unlearn—prioritizing other people's opinions and happiness at the expense of my own.

4

If the Shoe Fits

Once it became impossible to keep up the back-and-forth from New York, my mom and I rented a place full-time in Los Angeles. I was more than ready to start a new life, but I was also leaving my old life behind, and I didn't really understand the weight of what that sacrifice meant until it was already in the rearview mirror. We lived in a hotel for the first months, and my days were filled with homeschool, spending most of my free time with my mom. Looking back on this period, I never remember feeling lonely—my mom and I were best friends.

The longer I was in Los Angeles full-time, the more it felt like the world was at my fingertips. My follower count was growing faster than I could keep up with, and then suddenly everyone wanted to be my friend overnight. I was young and impressionable and easily swayed—and the lifestyle change alone is a lot on a still-developing brain. I'd be lying if I said it didn't go to my head. Without anyone to ground me, it was easy to get caught up in it all. And for a few years, I did.

But at the same time, missing my home in Long Island came in waves. I kept in touch with my friends, but sometimes that hurt even more than radio silence. Here I was, living every little girl's dream, yet simultaneously gutted at missing out on milestone moments like homecoming, prom, and graduation. I missed my best friends' birthdays because I was too busy to fly back home. No matter how hard I tried to cling to all the normal parts of being a teenager, it was impossible to balance everything, and in the end, work always won out.

As I got older and living in Los Angeles slowly shed more and more of its novelty, I started growing frustrated. The city that I'd romanticized for years gradually began revealing its darker side to me. Fancy events lost their luster, fake friends weeded their way out of my life, and I started feeling even more at odds with my career.

I didn't understand why, at the time, just that it always felt uncomfortable to sing songs that someone else wrote for me—that going onstage and performing them in front of an audience didn't feel right. I started putting more and more distance between myself and the "Madison Beer" image being put on display for the public. At times I almost felt embarrassed of it.

Shortly after the release of my first single, "Melodies," I went back to Long Island to go to a friend's birthday party. It was amazing to be back home for a week or two with familiar faces, but at the party I felt a huge shift for the first time. In LA I had been recognized and asked for photos a handful of times, but I guess in my head Long Island felt like home—the place where I am Madison and nothing else. Minutes after walking in, so many people I hadn't seen in years came up to me, taking selfies, asking questions. At first it was fun. I enjoyed the attention I was receiving. But when someone took over the music and started playing my song over the speakers, I shrank. It felt like I was Alice and I was getting smaller by the second, while everyone around me pointed and laughed. I ran out, hysterical. I think feeling anything but proud and only embarrassed in that moment was truly eye-opening to me.

Despite this, I returned to LA and moved forward. I kept all the sour feelings to myself, like a dirty secret. I was terrified that I would come across as a spoiled brat, or that anyone would believe I was ungrateful for the amazing opportunities I was given. But it wasn't a matter of my ego. And it sure wasn't a matter of not wanting to put in hard work. I was busier than I'd ever been, working more hours than I had been before I lived in LA, but it felt fruitless.

In short, I was making music I didn't want to listen to. I was making music to gain an audience that I didn't want. If I was putting all this work in to build a name for myself, was it even worth it if the end product wasn't something I took pride in? Would my sacrifices be in vain?

On the day of my first fitting, my mom had told me to think of it as playing a character, but I didn't sign up to be an actress. I wanted to be a singer—an *artist*—because I wanted to be *myself*. But now my career felt more like I was pretending to be someone else.

As I got older, the split only grew. And especially once my audience started to expand, I felt as if I was lying to them about who I was. Like I was an advertisement only meant to sell them something. I read their praise and felt like they were talking about someone else, like they loved a version of me that didn't even exist.

There's a psychological term for it: *role confusion*. In the pivotal teenage years where we're coming into our own, developing a sense of self, we try on different identities, experimenting with different hobbies and interests. If there are any obstacles in developing a solid sense of identity in those years, we're more likely to struggle for the rest of our lives. Teenagers who aren't able to explore their identity in safe ways have emotional, social, and psychological setbacks as adults.[*]

In my case, I was actively splitting my identity between the private and public spheres. For a normal teenager, choosing your college and major is the first step in solidifying a career path, which usually happens when you're around eighteen, still young, but with a handful of solid years to try things on for size. Meanwhile, I was barely fifteen and locked into a full *career*—one that required a very specific personality type in order to thrive. Sometimes I had to build my identity around my career, instead of the other way around.

---

[*] Kendra Cherry, "How People Develop an Identity or Cope with Role Confusion," Verywell Mind, June 22, 2022, https://www.verywellmind.com/identity-versus -confusion-2795735.

5

Mob Mentality

By the time I was sixteen, I had been receiving death threats and consistent hateful messages for four consecutive years. It had really started to weigh me down, and I remember the tipping point very clearly.

At the time, I had just started dating a boy who was more popular than me online. He had a huge fan base of really dedicated, passionate fans—most of them teenage girls who idolized him to an extreme, making it impossible for him to do any wrong. Predictably, once they found out that one of their beloved idols had a new girlfriend, they didn't exactly receive me with open arms.

I'd obviously dealt with hate before, but this backlash was completely different. The only "crime" I'd committed, in their eyes, was being at the receiving end of my boyfriend's affection.

The hate was overwhelming. And constant.

I was called endless names—labeled a whore for having him as my boyfriend, for dressing a certain way, for the most insignificant pieces of my personality. I was told he was doing charity work by dating me, that he could do so much better, that it was only a matter of time before he got bored of me and moved on to someone else.

Having doubts in a relationship is normal, being insecure is human, but hearing your own worst fears from someone else's mouth is excruciating. I wish I could say it didn't affect our relationship, but his fans' words cut deep, and I was already insecure enough. Hearing it over and over again only perpetuated my already underlying issues, regardless of him.

But I stuck it out. And when they realized hate didn't scare me away, their tactics changed. They started trying to spread rumors about me to bash my reputation. One of the most prominent was that I'd gotten with every other boy in his friend group before him—that I was a sex-addicted slut and had hooked up with every single one of his friends. Meanwhile, I had only ever kissed a few boys prior, and having my nonexistent sex life speculated on made me feel overexposed and uncomfortable. I didn't like seeing it, and I didn't like the thought of any of my guy friends seeing it and thinking of me in that light, either.

And regardless, what does it matter even if it were true? Realizing very young that women and men are treated so differently when it comes to being sexual is a tough pill to swallow, especially when it is made so public. From so young I was made to feel like I wasn't interesting enough on my own—that all men would ever want from me was sex. Objectified from the start, I was being taught to lean into it, only confirming what I'd already internalized in early childhood.

I've never spoken about what I am about to say publicly, and even though I have so much to say about it, the reason it's not a major topic in this book is because I'm still learning to be patient with myself and put my healing first. It is not a part of my story that deserves to be ignored, but I don't think I'm ready to go into too much detail. Quite simply, the boyfriend I am referring to was the first person to ever touch me consensually. I was sexually assaulted as a child and then again between fourteen and fifteen years old at a party in LA. The trauma from those incidents still affects me daily. I believe it will be a part of me forever. Regardless of this, it was all so overwhelming and upsetting, and no matter what traumas I had endured, nobody, not even my boyfriend, knew about them. You can see why these comments affected me so deeply.

When I got brought on as the opening act for my boyfriend's concert, I was riddled with anxiety on the days leading up to the performance. I was only supposed to go onstage for fifteen minutes and sing a few songs to start the show, but my nerves were worse than they had been for any other performance.

I did everything I could to brush it off. I avoided thinking about it altogether, but it caught up to me the night before the performance, once I was back in my hotel room by myself with nothing to distract me from my thoughts.

I regretted accepting the offer in the first place—whose idea was it to let me perform to a crowd full of kids who all hated me? What kind of idiot would agree to that? I saw all the possible outcomes, and none of them were positive. I could handle the crowd not knowing the words to my songs, sure, but I was convinced I would be booed off the stage, at the very least. No one wants to stand in front of a crowd of people who they know already dislike them. I was genuinely scared for my safety.

I called my mom, and something about hearing her voice when she picked up made all my anxiety spill forward. I burst into tears.

"Madison, what is going on? What's wrong?" She was understandably confused, and having her sixteen-year-old daughter call her inconsolable from states away probably made her assume all the worst-case scenarios.

"I can't do it," I managed through my tears, standing up and pacing the small hotel room. "You have to call my manager, tell him this was a stupid fucking idea, I can't go onstage tomorrow. I refuse."

"Madison, why? What happened?"

"Nothing happened, Mom, but they all hate me. They all hate me so much." I stopped at the window and drew the curtains open, looking down at the empty street below. If there had been a crowd outside the hotel with torches and pitchforks, I wouldn't have been surprised. When you're that young, and so much of your life is spent online, mass amounts of hate sometimes make it feel like the entire world is against you. It was hard to put things into perspective.

"Mad . . ." She sighed. "They wouldn't have asked you to perform if they thought it would be catastrophic. They're just a bunch of mean and jealous people who wish they were in your place."

I heard that argument a lot—*jealousy*. But I didn't like that it was used in a way to excuse people saying such hurtful things about me. What was I supposed to do? Give up every opportunity that was given to me because other people wanted it? Break up with my boyfriend because someone else wanted to date him? It didn't make sense. And it didn't make me feel any better.

"I don't want to do it, Mom. I'm not doing it," I insisted, panic rising in my chest. The lump in my throat was painful.

"You've performed to bigger crowds, Madison. You've sung a cappella in a room full of adults who had no idea who you were. Why is *this* the show that's getting you this worked up?"

"Because they all *despise* me," I emphasized, my voice growing thin in my desperation. I didn't know how else to explain it to her. It felt like she didn't understand the internet, how eager people were to find something to hold against me. "I'm scared they'll boo me offstage, and they'll take videos, and it'll be all over Twitter, I'll be a laughingstock—"

I stumbled over my words as I rambled, my thoughts spiraling.

We stayed on the phone for a long time. I was frightened. She tried so hard to encourage me and help me realize that it would all be okay.

"I think you should go out and hold your head high. I think you got this, but if you want to back out, I will support your choice. You're going to have to be the one who tells your manager, though," my mom said. "You need to explain all this to yourself. I can't be the middleman."

"You don't get it, goodbye," I muttered frustratedly. I couldn't stand it. My own mother didn't understand where I was coming from. I felt so alone. I knew I wasn't being dramatic or unreasonable, but I also knew—as much as the crowd scared me—that I couldn't muster up the courage to call my manager and back out at the last minute. Not the night before, not when I'd already flown out here for the occasion. My mom was giving me tough love, but she was right.

There were moments where I needed to face my fears head-on and push through despite my anxiety, and this was one of them. Everyone already knew I was scheduled as the opening act. If I backed out, it would have to be announced publicly, and that would give everyone an open invitation to speculate why. I didn't want to give any of the haters more of a reason to dislike me, to call me unprofessional, or spread rumors that I backed out of performing because I was scared. I needed to swallow my pride and get it over with. Still, I didn't get much sleep that night.

But when the day of the performance came, I stepped out onstage and no one booed. People clapped and cheered. There were a few unfriendly faces in the crowd, sure. But all the nightmare scenarios I'd spent hours playing out didn't happen.

What really helped ground me was seeing that the people in the audience were *real people*. Online, when they could hide behind a profile picture and a fake name, they seemed so much more intimidating. Looking out at that crowd helped put things into perspective.

I got offstage mostly happy to have gotten it over with—but also feeling a little embarrassed with myself for how much time I'd wasted the night before, turning today into a nightmare.

One of my favorite quotes is simply "Your anxiety is lying to you." I try to keep a mental list of all the times where I've proven my anxiety wrong, so I can look back at them when I'm in that same anxiety-blinded headspace. I use it as a way of rewiring my brain.

I think there's a healthy balance between challenging your

anxiety and pushing yourself into a situation you can't handle, but when I feel like it's manageable, I continue to seek out situations that will stretch the boundaries of my comfort zone.

For me, it's about being aware of where that comfort zone is, exactly where it ends, and making the conscious decision to do something to step outside of it, while also having the comfort of a safe way out if it gets too overwhelming.

I set small goals, just to prove to my brain and my body that positive experiences can come from facing your fears. If I'm scared about going to a party with a bunch of people I don't know, I try to make it a mission to have a good conversation with one stranger, to walk away from the night with at least *one* positive memory—so the next time I enter a room full of strangers I can say to myself: *Hey, the last time you did this, you made a friend.* These are small victories, but they are victories regardless.

And now, whenever I have a crowd that I'm scared to perform to, I think back to that moment and remember how shocked I was that it went positively. And I use it to combat my anxiety. Repeating that pattern over and over has helped retrain my brain from assuming every new situation will end in the worst-case scenario. And even when things don't turn out the way I want—where I might be slightly uncomfortable or embarrassed—no sour moment is ever anything close to the nightmare disasters my anxiety builds them up to be in my head.

Untangling Anxiety

Tell me about a time that your anxiety was proven wrong. Hold on to it. Is there something you're anxious about now that you could try and combat in a manageable, healthy way? If so, then what? Understanding the root of our anxieties detail by detail, broken down, in my experience, can help a lot. Deconstruct it. Prove it WRONG.

6

It's Not Me; It's You

Out of everything I went through as a result of my sudden rise to fame, having my private nude photos leaked at fifteen was one of the most traumatizing.

It still haunts me almost a decade later. Every time I think I'm fully healed, another side effect rears its ugly head, like peeling back the layers of an onion, and I realize just how much the trauma has leaked into every aspect of my life.

It started when I was Snapchatting a boy who was a childhood friend of mine. I'd known him for years, trusted him wholeheartedly, and we both had massive crushes on each other. We'd send videos and pictures back and forth—both of us young and still figuring out our bodies and sexualities. I thought it was impossible to screenshot or save a video through Snapchat. Once he saw it, it would be deleted forever. Plus, like I said, I *trusted* him.

Eventually, as most teenagers do, we grew apart. Months passed, and I thought nothing of it. At this point I was already living in LA, but I kept in contact with him and a handful of my friends from Long Island, which is how I first found out that there was a video of me being spread around my old school.

It happened in the span of a night. I remember it vividly, and wish I could forget. Every detail is burned into my brain. My mom had already gone to sleep, and I was lying in bed, absentmindedly scrolling through my phone. I was already nervous about dance practice the next morning, and I was trying to distract myself, knowing I needed to go to bed soon to wake up in time.

And then, out of nowhere, I got a text from a friend back home: yo, someone just added me to a group chat and sent a video of you holding your boobs.

I thought it was a joke at first, but then I started getting more and more texts from old classmates telling me they'd seen it. Most of them were from concerned friends, but a few of them were already poking fun at me, asking roundabout questions that all boiled down to: *Why were you careless enough to send the video in the first place?* My heart was pounding, and when one of my friends sent a screenshot of the video, my entire body went numb. It *was* me. And it was a video I'd sent to that boy. I had no idea how he'd saved a copy of it. Panic ensued.

It all happened so fast. One minute I was dozing off watching YouTube videos, and the next I was sobbing alone in my bedroom.

I called the boy I'd sent the video to, but he vehemently denied having a copy. I felt crazy. He acted just as shocked as I was that it had gotten out, but who else could have done it? He was the only one I sent it to. I hung up on him and pleaded with my friends to tell everyone else to delete it.

But beyond that, I didn't know what else to do. It was already being sent around, and I was powerless. It was humiliating enough to know my closest friends had seen these videos, but I was also terrified that someone might send them to my parents, and they'd ground me for the rest of my life, or somehow my little brother would hear about it. The thought made me sick.

In a matter of minutes, as the reality of what was happening sank in, my goal changed from stopping the video from being spread around my old school to stopping it from reaching social media.

Deep down, I knew it was a matter of time. All it would take was for one person to post it online—knowing I had a growing following, knowing how something like this could shatter my reputation—and it would spread like wildfire. Once it reached the internet, it wouldn't disappear. It would live there forever.

I had to be up for dance in a few hours, and most of my friends who were helping me track down the video had already fallen asleep. I was too scared to wake up my mom, so I had no other choice but to turn my phone over, shove it under my pillow, and try to go to bed, hoping that the nightmare would be over in the morning.

But I couldn't sleep. I couldn't get my heart to slow down, and my brain was running on overdrive. When I felt my phone ringing, the shrill ringtone cut right through me, and I rolled over to check the caller ID. It was my friend in Florida.

"Hello?" I sat up, my voice shaking.

"Hey . . ." My friend seemed hesitant. "So . . . there's this video . . ."

"I know," I cut her off, nervous and on edge. "Everyone at my old school has it. Did someone send it to you?"

"Yeah." She seemed relieved that she didn't have to be the one to break the news to me. "A bunch of kids at my school just got sent it, too."

Tears stung at my eyes all over again. It had started in Long Island and somehow gotten sent all the way to a high school in Florida. I had no control.

"Can you please tell them not to post it or share it?" I begged her, trying not to sound like I was crying. "My . . . my team is already on it. The person who sent it out is going to get arrested."

It was a weak lie, but it was the only thing I could think of, hoping it would scare everyone into deleting the video and pretending they'd never even seen it.

From that point on, it became a waiting game. I slept restlessly and kept waking up to more texts from people who had the video, but it hadn't yet reached the internet.

I was waiting outside my house for my mom to pick me up for dance class when I saw the first tweet: follow and dm me for madison beer's nudes.

It was starting. Someone I had never seen—someone who I didn't know—had the video. And they were using it for followers and attention.

I messaged them instantly, begging, please delete your tweet and please dont send it to anyone, please im just a kid who made a stupid mistake.

The account blocked me immediately. I sat staring at their page with the username now dull, unable to refresh their tweets. I was powerless.

It was during dance rehearsals that the video finally made its way online. Someone posted it to Vine, and it had already been picked up on Twitter and Instagram. It was being shared over and over until it became a trending topic. I flipped my phone over, saw the barrage of texts, and broke down.

It felt like my life was over. All I could think about was the internet safety lesson in middle school, where our librarian sat our class down and warned us about the dangers of the internet, making us believe that if we posted anything inappropriate— like tweeting about being drunk—our future employers would see and wouldn't want to hire us.

That was laughable compared to this.

I sobbed on the floor of the dance studio, glued to my phone. I could only watch as the video spread farther and farther, reading every single comment about how disgusting I was, how my career was over, how my parents must be so ashamed of me. People were criticizing my body and pointing out every single flaw. This marked one of the first major instances where it felt like the only way out—the only way this would ever end—was to take my own life.

The humiliation only snowballed. The sentiments being tweeted were the same things I heard from my parents and managers when they found out what had happened. Everyone was upset with me. Ashamed. Telling my parents the truth was mortifying enough, but it was just as crushing to hear how disappointed my team was. I was fifteen years old, being made to feel like my one mistake would not only cost me my entire career and future but also ruin the reputations of all the people who worked on my team.

All I wanted to do was lock myself in my room and hide under the covers. I didn't even want to look at myself in the mirror or change out of the clothes I was wearing. I felt violated. I became suspicious of everyone in my life. Who else could possibly have photos or videos of me that they'd post online, even if they weren't explicit? I smoked a cigarette once at a sleepover—what if someone had taken a video? I couldn't trust anyone, and no one was sticking up for me. No one wanted to hear my side. I'd ruined my life, somehow, with one single ten-second video.

Facing my parents, specifically my dad, was horrific. I will never forget his face when I got home—my parents had never looked at me that way before. For the rest of the day I couldn't look my dad in the eyes. The three of us sat on my mom's bed, my manager on the phone, discussing what our next steps would be. My dad buried his face in his hands, rubbing his temples every time my manager spoke. It felt endless.

When we went out to dinner later that week, my mom parked the car, but I couldn't bring myself to step out. It felt like every person who passed by us on the street was staring at me, as if *everyone* had seen the video, as if it was plastered on a billboard in the middle of Times Square. I kept my head down and walked as quickly as I could into the restaurant.

It's hard to remember the specifics of the days that followed, but what I do remember, word for word, are the countless hateful comments I read. I spent more time with my eyes glued to my phone than I did in the real world.

Not only was I embarrassed and ashamed and insecure about my body, but now I had to suffer through awkward conversations with my team about how to do damage control. Sitting across the table from my mom and my managers, knowing they'd seen the video, knowing they were disappointed in me, only drilled the shame that much deeper into my being.

My team advised me to vehemently deny that it was me in the video. At the time it seemed like our only option. Because my entire face wasn't in it, the hope was that if I denied it once, publicly, and then pretended to be blissfully unaware that the video was continuing to spread, the speculation would eventually die down and I could move on.

But that didn't happen right away. Instead, denying it was me in the video only fanned the flames further, and people started trying to prove I was lying. They posted pictures comparing my manicure in the video to my manicure on my Instagram posts, or comparing the headboard of my bed to the headboard in the videos. Even something as specific as the freckles on my body was put up for debate. Seeing my body being dissected online, over and over, made me want to shed my skin, crawl inside myself, and never come out.

To make matters worse, other videos started surfacing, ones that weren't of me but of girls that looked enough like me that it was believable. They were much more explicit than mine, but because they were grouped in with the first video, people thought nothing of believing they were me, too. There was no way I could come out and say, "*This* video is real, but *these* aren't," so my only choice was to deny, deny, deny.

So many people had been waiting for a chance to jump at me, and the leaked videos allowed them to reduce me to one thing: a slut, a whore, a stupid little girl who didn't deserve the platform she'd been given. No one was protecting me. No one was putting a buffer between me and the fallout. I was front and center, taking all the blame and responsibility.

Without any other options, the only thing I could do was wait it out—wait for people to get bored of the drama and move on to the next online scandal. I hoped it would be that simple, but really, even when it did cool down online, it reversed none of the damage that had been inflicted on me.

In the aftermath, the hardest part for me to digest was the fact that no one showed up for an underage girl who'd had her privacy violated so ruthlessly. I scoured the internet trying to find *one* person sticking up for me, just for some sort of comfort—some sort of confirmation that I wasn't entirely in the wrong. I found nothing. Not one person felt bad that I'd had my trust betrayed. Not one person reached out and reassured me that it wasn't my fault. No one stood up and said, "Hey, maybe this reaction is wrong, and she is only human." It was only wave after wave of shame.

I'd endured hate online for a few years by that point, like I said, but now I was even more confused about how much of a punishment I really deserved. Was I really disgusting for what I did? I knew sending the videos wasn't a good idea, but was I really irredeemable?

Was this something no one else had ever done before? Was there something wrong with me?

In the end, I was the one who paid the price. People were committing criminal offenses by spreading child pornography of me online, and yet I was the one who had to hire someone to take it down. Almost all the money I'd saved working so far now had to be put toward paying an internet sheriff to erase the video from the internet. That act alone only drilled it more into my head—it was my fault. I was paying this price because it was my fault. Right?

I spent countless sleepless nights digging through social media, sending link after link to the internet sheriff to make sure they were taken down. But that also meant I saw *everything*. I saw group chats where people made fun of me, laughing at the backlash I was getting. I found online groups of grown men making lewd, violent sexual comments about me, using vocabulary I barely even knew. I even saw a video of a man who appeared to be well into his forties masturbating to the video. To say I was disturbed is an understatement. Grown adults commenting on the body of an underage girl is gross in general, yet no one seemed to raise a red flag.

To this day I find myself scratching my head. How was this a trending topic on Twitter? How did I scroll through thousands and thousands of tweets about a leaked video of a fifteen-year-old girl without seeing *one* person say that was a problem? Half of the people weren't even being mean, they were joking. It was a big joke, and I was at the center of it. But all these years later, there's nothing funny about it.

I didn't know it at the time, but it's indicative of a bigger problem. Misogyny is woven so deeply into our society that everyone's first reaction was to be disgusted by me—by the fact that a young girl would even *think* of exploring her sexuality. If I was a boy, it would have been different. The reaction would have been, "Oh god, poor kid, he must be so embarrassed." If I was a boy and it was a girl who leaked the video of me, *she* would be the one blamed—called psycho, manipulative, and vindictive.

If I was a boy, I would have been shielded from the consequences of my actions and allowed to move on from my mistake. But I was a girl, and I wasn't allowed to be sexual, even when all of my friends were doing the same thing behind closed doors.

Yes, I was underage. I was young, and that's what complicates it. But developmental psychology agrees that early adolescence is when we start exploring our sexuality.* By those standards, I was progressing age-appropriately by doing something as simple as having curiosity about my own body. Sending the video to a boy wasn't the best idea, but that's not what people were mad about. They were shocked that I—a female—was expressing any sort of sexual autonomy.

No one's rage was coming from a place of concern. None of the backlash online was to protect me from being exploited, or to educate me about sexual health, consent, or internet safety. No, I was being shamed for being sexual in general. My peers were making fun of me for trying to be "sexy." People were joking about something that was so traumatic for me. And it was even more difficult as a young girl with past sexual traumas. I'd already had my bodily autonomy and my trust betrayed, and now here it was again, being broadcast for the world to see.

At the end of the day, I should have been protected. And if I had been, it would have saved me years of damage. Instead, I faced the harsh reality of internalized misogyny and what it means to be female in a world that prioritizes male sexual desire.

---

* "Childhood Sexual Development," National Center on the Sexual Behavior of Youth, accessed July 8, 2022, https://www.ncsby.org/content/childhood-sexual -development.

Dear Madison,

Do you ever have to deal with haters in real life? You speak openly about dealing with hate online, but how do you navigate it when you're confronted face-to-face?

Natalie, Wyoming

Back when I was first signed with my label, I didn't understand how much of a divide there was between the online world and the real one. I was having a hard time coping with the sudden flood of unwanted opinions about me—on my voice, the way I dressed, my personality. It was overwhelming, and I was nowhere near prepared for it. When I received hate online, it hurt just as much as someone saying it to my face.

The more my platform grew, the more I feared setting foot outside my house and running into one of these people in real life. When I got approached in public, I was more apt to believe that the person was a hater, as opposed to assuming they were a fan coming up to ask for a picture. I held my breath, waiting for the moment when someone took the opportunity to tell me these awful things in person. I dreaded the thought that I'd have nowhere to run and hide. It wouldn't be like a comment I could pretend I didn't see.

No one else around me knew what it was like. I didn't have anyone I could talk to about it who truly understood. None of my friends had been in my position, and while my mom tried her best to sympathize, there was still a gap in our understanding. Plus it was embarrassing to open up about it. I'd started believing some of the negative things I was told, so I feared telling my friends the specifics of what I received hate for and having them tell me, "Well, I mean, they're kind of right."

So I kept it to myself like some sort of awful secret, hoping if I ignored it for long enough it would go away. But it didn't. My platform continued to grow, and it only got worse.

After my nudes leaked, I spent even more time keeping track of what everyone was saying about me. I had a newfound fear of the videos and pictures resurfacing, so I took it upon myself to track all my social media, to search up my name, and make sure no one started circulating them again. I figured as long as I knew what people were saying about me, I had some sort of control over it. (This, of course, wasn't true.)

It interfered with my daily life—I struggled to be present in any interaction without getting caught up in my phone.

"Earth to Madison," my manager called across the room, waving his hand to get my attention. I snapped out of my daze, blinking a few times and looking up to find the rest of my team staring at me. Guilty, I locked my phone.

"Sorry." I sighed. "What were you saying?"

"What's up with you?"

"People are just fucking mean," I muttered, tossing my phone to the other side of the couch before I could get caught up in scrolling again. I wanted it as far away from me as possible. "I hate doing interviews. I can't do anything right. Every time I open my mouth, someone finds something wrong with it."

"Go to the grocery store," he told me. I just stared at him in confusion.

"What?" I was defensive at first. Had he even heard what I said?

"I'm serious." He laughed at my confusion. "Go to the grocery store. No one's going to look at you, no one's going to care, no one's going to hate on you, and no one's going to say anything to you."

At first it felt dismissive—as if he was saying the bullying didn't matter. I was too quick to write him off, thinking he had no idea what he was talking about, that he'd never experienced it for himself.

But it stuck with me for the next few days. I thought more about it, and the next time we went out in public, I remembered his words. My mom dragged me to the mall on the weekend, despite my protests that I'd rather stay home, and I trailed behind her as we walked through crowds of people. My anxiety was getting the best of me—I was still in the mindset where I was convinced everyone hated me.

Annoyed, I sat on a bench outside a store while my mom took her time browsing. I bent my knees up to my chest and stayed quiet, tucked back behind a large potted plant, and watched as people passed by.

As boredom set in, I started studying people's faces. A little boy in a superhero costume. An old couple holding hands. A group of teenage girls in soccer uniforms.

It's like I was waiting for all of them to realize who I was—like a scene out of a horror movie. All of their eyes would turn to me, and they'd think, *Oh, god, that's her. That's the girl.* I braced myself for that moment, but it never came. In reality, a handful of people glanced at me in passing, but no one seemed to have any idea who I was.

My manager wasn't trying to insult me, I realized. He was only trying to put things into perspective—to remind me that there's an entire world outside of the internet. It was humbling (and strangely comforting) to realize that no one really cared who I was. I was just another grumpy teenage girl waiting for her mom outside a clothing store.

I was so scared of everyone knowing all my darkest secrets. But a handful of kids on the internet wasn't representative of the entire world. I could exist in this world—the real one—and not have to wait for the other shoe to drop.

The truth is, even though I could go on for days about every negative comment I've read that's hurt my feelings, I can count on one hand the times I've encountered that same energy in real life, if that. Ninety-nine percent of the time, the people spewing hatred online would never *dare* say it to my face. And I've realized this more and more as I've gotten older.

In 2021 Twitter had around 300 million active users. Alone, that number is terrifying. But compared to Earth's population— 7.8 billion—it's a speck of dust. Barely 4 percent of the world uses Twitter. I try to remind myself of this whenever I'm feeling overwhelmed with negativity online. When I get hate, I'm dealing with a fraction of a fraction of a fraction of the world. Not to say that makes it okay, but it's helpful to be able to put it in perspective. It makes the online world feel less intimidating.

I have a scary good memory when it comes to names and

faces. There've been a few occasions where I've met someone, recognized them from Twitter, and remembered seeing their tweets criticizing me. I keep it to myself, but it's always amusing (and slightly cathartic) to watch the same person online who made fun of my fashion sense say the exact opposite to me in person.

At the end of the day, it's easy to be bold online when you never have to take accountability for your own actions. It's easy to be flippant with your words when you assume the person on the other end will never see them. For most people, it's like shouting into the void.

On the other hand, when we meet face-to-face, both of us have to acknowledge that we're human beings. And if you were to say those same insults to me in person, you'd have to deal with the consequences—you'd have to see it hurt my feelings, and you'd have to answer for your words if I chose to ask you, "Why do you think it's okay to say something like that?"

Moral of the story: kindness is cool. You don't need to send hate to someone just because you have a social media account. Realizing that your words are powerful and should be used carefully is a beautiful thing.

7

Blessing in Disguise

When I was sixteen, my label and manager let me go.

It felt like a long-overdue breakup. It was an amicable split. But no matter how gently I was let down, I still felt like a failure—like I'd uprooted my entire family and moved to LA just to end up right back where we started.

I also lost a team of people around me who I thought were family. I had worked with them for years, only to be dropped and never hear from most of them again. I felt abandoned. And I felt like a cash cow—used to make money and then tossed aside the second I wasn't good enough anymore. It was a lot to process at sixteen years old. I believed I'd fumbled my one shot at my dream, and I'd spend the rest of my life regretting it.

Even though no one explicitly connected the two, I felt a large part of this was due to the nudes incident. It solidified the shame even more, proving my worst fear—that it would leak into every aspect of my life. I sent a video to a boy I had a crush on, and now I'd lost my entire career as a result of it.

"Maybe this is a blessing in disguise," my mom told me one night, sitting on the edge of my bed. We'd been in a weird limbo for about a week, still in Los Angeles but stuck on what to do next. She could tell I was dealing with a lot—I was quieter than usual, spending more time in my room, feeling like I'd lost all sense of purpose.

"It doesn't feel like it," I admitted. I looked at her and felt incredibly guilty. She'd given up her own business to move out with me to Los Angeles, believed in me wholeheartedly, and I'd failed her. I put an enormous amount of responsibility on myself at that age. Probably more than I should have.

"Nothing's changed, Madison." She moved closer. "Your fans didn't abandon you. You didn't lose your voice. You're still as talented and creative as you were on day one, aren't you?"

I shrugged. She sighed heavily.

"Listen, this is entirely your decision," she told me. "Don't worry about me, or what I think, or the work it means I have to do. If you want to keep going, I'm behind you one hundred percent, and we'll stay here and figure this out. But that means we're going to have to work our asses off.

"But"—her voice softened—"if this is too much for you, maybe this is a blessing in disguise. We can go back to Long Island, we'll enroll you in school again, and singing can just be your hobby. You'll still be able to post singing videos for your fans."

My thoughts were racing so fast, I had to fight to focus on her words. I was avoiding the decision for as long as I could, and it was hard to hear it laid out for me so plainly.

"Going home doesn't mean you failed, either. But this is your decision, Madison," she told me, "because I can't force you either way. You have to really sit with yourself and figure out what you want to do."

"Okay," was all I could manage at first, retreating into my head as I pieced it all together.

I knew going back home didn't mean I was giving up. For me, it was more about deciding if I still loved this enough—loved *music* enough—that I was willing to put my all into it, to dive in headfirst. I was so young when this all began that I didn't realize I was making lifelong decisions.

Now I was older, and I knew exactly what it took. I needed to decide if I even liked what I was doing anymore, or if I was only continuing because I was caught up in the momentum—if I was only going through the motions because I thought it was what I *had* to do.

No matter how amazing and gratifying it was, I had lost a large chunk of my childhood to this. I was forced to watch all my best hometown friends grow closer and start high school without me. I gave up a normal school experience, life moments like prom and homecoming, and all the summers I begged to go back to camp but never found the time. Going home meant I could regain some of the normalcy I lost. I'd be lying if I said it wasn't appealing.

But my mom was right. Being dropped wasn't the end of everything. I still had a large following that didn't hinge on whether or not I had a label backing me. And even if my old team hadn't seen my potential, did that mean no one else in the world would? Why would I write myself off before I even gave myself a chance?

So maybe it was a blessing in disguise. For a long time I had been trying to fit into someone else's mold for me, but now the mold itself was gone. I needed to grow into myself again. I'd have to figure out who I was as an artist on my own, but as intimidating as it felt, it was also exciting. I owed it to myself to at least try.

While negotiating the details of going independent was rocky, the emotional turmoil of being dropped was harder to work through. It wasn't just a bump in my career—it was a hit to my personal life, too. Coupled with the trauma of having my nudes leaked, it completely shattered the image I had of Los Angeles and the industry. These two big, life-altering events happening back to back knocked me off my feet, tilted my world on its axis, and left me feeling like I had no idea who I was. I didn't know who I could trust anymore, and I didn't even know I needed to seek help for the way I was feeling.

It was a lot of conflicting emotions for a newly sixteen-year-old girl to try to shoulder on her own. I felt like I was my own worst enemy. I retreated more and more into myself, and it was the beginning of some of the darkest years of my life, starting at age sixteen and following me into my twenties. There were many times—just like the night my nudes were leaked—that I felt so backed into a corner I thought the only way out was to end my life.

Once, on a particularly heavy day, I climbed over the edge of my balcony in LA and stood there, a million thoughts running through my head as I stared down at the ground, my eyes going in and out of focus. I don't think I would have jumped. It was more about knowing that I could—that I had a way out if it became too much. Still, I lingered there for a long while, chilled by the fact that I wasn't all that scared of being up so high.

My little brother found me and screamed for my parents, and

as I climbed back over, listening to them all freak out, I was only confused why they were making such a big deal out of it. The thought of killing myself was so normal to me at that point that I had forgotten it wasn't something everyone pondered on a daily basis.

As for my career, starting over again was terrifying.

Even though I was eager to try, rebuilding my confidence after being dropped was a long and difficult process. I was a starry-eyed, naive girl when I first came out to Los Angeles, and as my mom and I started facing the industry on our own, I realized just how much of my blind confidence I'd lost. I went from having the support of an entire professional team and photo shoots on huge, shiny sets to shooting the cover for my next single with a hand-held camera in my living room.

Not only was I starting over, but it felt like I was buried six feet under—like I had to dig myself back up to the surface first, and only *then* would I have a shot at a dream. Before, I'd been so excited to offer up new ideas and collaborate, but now, even though I had so many things I wanted to try, I wrote myself off before I even got a chance to voice them. I was well into my teenage years and plagued with insecurity, shouldering years of negative comments that made me believe I wasn't good enough to be taken seriously.

In rebranding myself, I wanted to move as far away from my "old" image as possible. I wanted my entrance back into the music world to be jarring enough that people would have to take me seriously. It was a big deal to reintroduce myself after being dropped by my label. There were a lot of eyes on me.

Ironically enough, as I began to slip into some of my darkest years, I was in the midst of rebranding myself as a strong, bad-ass independent female. It felt like the biggest diversion from the sweet bubblegum pop image I had before. I wanted to be a solid, empowering role model for my audience, but in reality I felt anything but.

My EP *As She Pleases* was the first step in rebuilding some of my confidence. I still cherish those songs and all they taught me. The title speaks for itself. It was my first try at writing my own music, and all I wanted to do was make music that I liked—it was that simple. In the beginning, writing my own music and becoming more involved in the production process was scary. The reckless confidence I had when I initially started in this industry had been worn down. When I'd tried to give creative input before, I was always shot down, made to feel like it was something I should leave up to the experts. I was terrified of being rejected, of not being good enough.

It took years before I could proudly call myself a songwriter. But the most amazing part about gaining confidence as an artist was finally feeling like my music was resonating with my listeners. I was actually putting out music I was proud of. After bending myself to other people's wills for so many years, I was doing as I pleased, slowly discovering myself and my own sound independent of outside opinion. I had a long road ahead, but I was taking steps in the right direction. A direction that felt bright.

Playlist of My Life

A song I connected with on my first listen:

A song that reminds me of my childhood:

A song that calms me down:

A song for driving with the windows down:

A song I know every word to:

A song that reminds me of my best friend:

A song that makes me feel less alone:

8

Inner Child

By the time I was nearing the end of my teenage years, I could barely remember what life was like before being signed, and my self-worth was made up entirely of other people's opinions about me.

When you're a kid, and the people around you tell you what you are, you believe them. And the traits that other people emphasize about you, you lean into. It's easy to put ourselves into those categories when we're young. While the praise we're given as children can push us to grow in healthy ways, sometimes the things we internalize as "valuable" aren't exactly healthy. For young girls, it starts when people in childhood praise us for being "cute," or "easygoing," or "well-behaved," and so we quietly begin to believe that those are the things we're supposed to be. Boys are praised for being "strong," "tough," and "manly," so they continue to do things that live up to those expectations.

Growing up, I was a cute kid and was always told so by people around me. And so—as anyone would—I learned that that was something I was valued for, something that would get me attention and approval, especially from adults and my peers. I learned to define myself by my beauty and my talent, because those seemed to be the things that everyone around me cared the most about.

The older I got, the more I shaped my personality around both of those things. But because I was so focused on being recognized in *other* people's eyes, I started moving further and further away from being able to recognize it on my own. I thought the only way to earn those labels was if someone else told me what I was. It didn't matter what I thought of myself.

My brother and I spent all of our childhood summers at sleep-away camp. I thrived there—I spent the entire school year counting down the days until camp started, until I could see my friends again. I woke up early every single morning just so I could cram as many activities as I could into my day. I loved it all—waterskiing, crafting, making new friends—but the highlight of my summers was always the plays we put on, where all of camp would be in the audience.

When I was ten years old and waiting eagerly for the cast list to be posted, practically pressing my nose to the paper as I traced my finger down the list of names, you can imagine my disappointment when I realized I didn't get the leading role I wanted.

Obviously, it was childish. But in the moment, it felt world-ending. And I couldn't quite figure out *what* I was feeling.

It might have been easier to write it off as jealousy, but it wasn't that simple. It was a sensation that cut a lot deeper. It had nothing to do with the girl who got the leading role, and everything to do with me. I thought my audition went smoothly. The judges had seemed impressed. What did I do wrong?

And then my thoughts started to spiral further. People valued me for the way I looked—had I not been pretty enough? Was I not a good enough singer? And—*oh my god*—what would happen if I wasn't talented anymore? If I lost it all, somehow?

Who was I without these things?

And because my singing and my appearance were the two things that I valued about myself—the two things that I thought made me worthy of other people's love—it hurt.

It was a moment of childish letdown in hindsight, but it speaks volumes about just how much emphasis I was taught to put on other people's opinions of me.

Once I was in the thick of my career, the highs and lows only got more and more extreme, and I started losing my ability to exist somewhere in the middle. Because my teenage years were spent online, because I always had access to other people's opinions of me, I never really got to develop my own idea of who I was in the same way I would have if I had had a normal teenage experience in my hometown. Part of it was just because I was a teenage girl trying to learn her place in the world, but it was heightened by the fact that I was thrown into the spotlight so quickly, so suddenly, that I never learned who I was without thousands of eyes on me. Sometimes I felt like I was performing to an audience, like I was on some *Truman Show*-esque reality show, even when I was completely alone in my bedroom.

I held so many conflicting views of who I was. Someone would tell me I was talented, destined for stardom, and I'd believe them. But then someone would tell me that my voice wasn't anything special, and I'd instantly switch into believing them, too. It was all blacks and whites. One day I would wake up and feel on top of the world, and the next day I would feel like an impostor in my own skin. I could never exist in a gray area.

Sometimes it was great. When I was being praised, I felt unstoppable, riding out a never-ending high. It felt like everyone loved me.

But because the internet is so fast-moving, because everyone's opinions are so rapidly changing, I never got to stay in the public's good graces for long. I was a young teenager who was still learning how to conduct herself as an adult, and every single one of my mistakes was broadcast for the world to see. Those periods where I felt I'd fallen from the public's good graces were dark.

Looking back, it's easy to see even through something as simple as my fashion sense. The clothing I wore was always changing in style. I went through a massive tomboy phase, and then a bubbly girly phase, and then a phase where I thought I only had to wear certain name brands. I was trying on different aesthetics to see what would stick, hoping one of them would feel right, but they never really did. I always felt a little bit like an impostor.

My shifting self-image became clear to me when I was alone, especially in the summer after my long-term boyfriend and I broke up for the first time, summer of 2017. It was the first time I had been truly single since I was fifteen, and no matter where I turned, I was reminded of him. On top of that, I was learning who I was without a partner for the first time in years.

One of the biggest changes in my thinking that helped me develop my own sense of self-worth—outside of social media— was figuring out where I was getting my validation from. Once it was clear to me that I couldn't keep on depending on other people to tell me who my true self was, that any praise would never be permanent and sustainable, I was lost on what to do.

It was a long process, and it's something I'm still working on, but now I've learned the best way to find stability is by keeping a safe distance between myself and the comments made about me by others—online or in real life. I need to be a whole person, secure in who I am, completely independent of whether or not anyone else loves or hates me. I can't let myself be shaken either way.

It's difficult to try and push aside the hate, but it's even harder not to become dependent on the positivity. It probably sounds weird, saying that I needed to learn how to "ignore" the positive comments. I'm forever grateful for the love I receive. It means the world to me. But I also can't let myself become too reliant on it, because I know how quickly the internet moves and how easily people can change their opinions. It isn't stable.

I think this can be said for everybody, not just me. Most of us have now grown up in a time when no matter who you are, where you're from, or what you do, sadly a lot of your popularity is based on a follower count. The amount of likes a photo of ourselves might get will reflect how we look in it. If it does bad, you must look bad. It is our simple (but flawed) logic. I think most of us are victims of it subconsciously. It isn't our fault, it is the system we have been raised in. But I do think that one day, even if it is far in the future, people will realize the severe damage that this has done to growing minds. We are teaching ourselves that our self-worth is inherently based on who else agrees.

But at the time, when I truly realized how I had lost touch with my innate sense of what I enjoyed, I floundered. I had built myself around what everyone else expected from me, defined myself by everyone else's comments on my appearance, my talent, my personality. I wanted to be seen for me, we all do. But first I had to see myself and understand what that meant—who this person was. I figured if I could love myself so unconditionally, with such certainty, it wouldn't matter if anyone else did. Without the internet's praise to draw from, I was forced to sit with myself and truly figure out who I was again. I had to build myself from the ground up.

Reconnecting with Your Inner Child

Sometimes, in the process of growing up, we fall out of touch with ourselves. It's important to try to reconnect with that inner child and all the things we loved instinctually, before the world told us who we had to be.

How did you define yourself as a child? As you've grown, how has that changed? Have you lost any interests or traits that you'd like to get back? What parts of yourself do you long to reconnect with? If you could write a letter to your inner child, what would you say?

9

High Tide

The summer of 2019 was simultaneously the lowest point of my personal life and the height of my creative career. It was a very transitional period—I was newly twenty, working on my album for hours a day, while also falling deeper and deeper into a pit of depression and anxiety. I was becoming more and more dependent on drugs like Xanax to sleep at night, and I was actively suicidal, but I had grown so used to it that the thought didn't alarm me anymore. I'd wake up, tell myself I'd rather not have, and continue on with my day. I titled my album *Life Support* because that's genuinely what it was—my lifeline. If I didn't have the studio to escape to during the day, I wouldn't have left my apartment at all.

The issues that began boiling under the surface after I started my career had only gotten worse as I got older. I struggled heavily with self-harming, but I was hurting myself in countless other ways too. I was abusive toward myself and allowed other people in my life to get away with that same behavior, simply because I felt like I deserved it.

Standing on the edge of my balcony years ago was a distant memory, but my outlook had only grown darker. I clung to the lingering thought that, inevitably, I would end up taking my own life. It had gotten to the point that I couldn't see any other way out.

Even my fans started catching on to the fact that something was wrong. When I was photographed in public, I was always in sweatpants, no makeup, and my arms were always covered, even on a hot and sunny day. People speculated online, and even though so much of it came from a place of genuine concern, it only made me want to lock myself in my apartment and never leave. I was making music and doing what I loved, but I was miserable, and on top of it all I felt guilty for feeling so depressed despite all the overwhelming positives in my life. This was supposed to be exciting—I was writing an album full of songs that I truly loved, starting to gain the creative freedom I'd always wanted. What more could I ask for? Why did I feel so wrong?

I spent a lot of time alone. My friend group was in flux, I didn't have many close friends, and even when they did make attempts to hang out with me, I clung to the familiar safety of my apartment. On a typical day I'd wake up, spend the day in the studio, and come home to an empty apartment, climbing straight into bed, taking Xanax, and wasting away hours on my phone.

The time alone left me with a lot of space to think. Up until that point, it felt like I'd been working nonstop from the time I was twelve. My career had moved so fast that I rarely had a chance to slow down and take it all in. If something traumatic happened, I had no time to process it. I just had to shoulder the pain and move on. I never allowed myself to be the victim. I always forced myself to swallow my tears, shake it off, and remind myself that there were a million other kids who would do anything to be in my position. But it was a really harmful view that I held. I invalidated my own pain by convincing myself it wasn't worthy of being called "pain" in the first place. And once I started having more time to reflect on this, my past caught up to me.

When I went to my friends for advice, they always seemed to start with "But remember, so many people love you!" Which is true, I know, but the love I felt from those people didn't mean the hurt I felt would disappear just like that. Both could exist at once.

And being loved by thousands didn't mean I loved myself. Not at all.

On one day in particular, I had just gotten out of a studio session and was waiting in line for food at a local restaurant. Standing there, I felt like I was floating somewhere outside my body, watching the world moving around me without actively participating in it. I kept my eyes on my phone and hoped no one recognized me. I didn't want to be seen, I didn't want to be "Madison Beer"—I just wanted to get my food and go home. I was nearly at the counter to order when I heard giggling from behind me.

Teenage girls can be scary. This was a time when my knee-jerk reaction was to believe the world was against me, and immediately I assumed the group of girls clustered in a circle around their table was making fun of me. I glanced up from my phone, accidentally made eye contact, and quickly looked away, pretending I hadn't seen them. I heard their hushed whispers—*"Wait, it's actually her"*—as they tried to work up the courage to come over and say hi. I looked up again, smiling hesitantly.

Thankfully, they weren't making fun of me, and one of them shyly waved back. Understanding that they wanted to say hi, I left my spot in line to walk over to their table and greet them, feeling I'd be rude if I didn't. As soon as the initial awkwardness faded, they started talking over each other, showering me with compliments, and I had to push aside my foggy mood to be present in the moment. I sat down at their table for a few minutes to talk.

"You have the best smile," one of them told me. "You look so happy, it's like you're glowing."

I almost laughed. I felt like I was accepting their compliments on behalf of someone else. It was hard to believe anything good they said about me when it felt so far from the truth. They saw me as someone so happy and confident and self-assured, when I was anything but.

Even after it was over, I couldn't get the interaction out of my head. Once I got home, I sat down on my couch and pulled up my Instagram, scrolling through my feed and trying to see myself through their eyes. I wanted so badly to love myself the way my fans seemed to love me.

It made more sense then. The last photo I posted was a red carpet photo in full glam makeup. A couple of posts before that: an announcement that I'd been signed to my new label. Two posts before: a music video teaser, a video of me laughing in the studio.

I wasn't posting videos of me crying, or pictures of me alone in my apartment high out of my mind while all my friends were out partying—I was portraying the best version of myself that I could, trying to fool everyone into thinking I was happy, busy, successful.

But I looked at the girl on the screen and saw a stranger. And it made me feel even more alone, because no one knew the real me. I was so good at keeping up appearances that no one knew how much I was struggling. Was I really that good of an actress?

If I took my own life, would no one have seen it coming?

I was so visible, yet so unseen. I felt the most isolated I'd ever been in my life, like I'd backed myself into a corner.

The truth is, even though I wouldn't change it, I'd lost a lot of my childhood to my career.

The truth is, there were a lot of things I wished the adults around me had done differently to protect me.

The truth is, I had so many things going right for me, and none of it was enough to cancel out that hurt.

I didn't know how to handle it. I didn't know how to let myself be sad, to feel those bad feelings, without trying to talk myself out of it. And it was like all the time I spent ignoring this—holding back wave after wave of past emotions—had only now caught up to me, and suddenly I was grieving it all at once. The wave finally broke, crashing over and flooding everything in my life, and I was drowning without any sign of shore.

My crisis point came amid a perfect storm. Sometime in late August, someone I was seeing broke up with me for another girl, I got into an argument with one of my close friends, and then—while I was scrolling through social media, trying to distract myself—my timeline was full of hate directed at me.

I felt like I was being attacked from all angles. The entire world hated me, and I hated me even more. I was so tired of fighting with myself. That night, after many nights of debating, I took a handful of whatever pills I could find and prayed that I wouldn't wake up in the morning.

When I did, what scared me the most was how apathetic I was. I was so numb that I couldn't even figure out whether I was disappointed or relieved that I had been unsuccessful. I couldn't remember anything that happened after I took the pills. Maybe, if this were a movie where everything works out in the end, that morning would have been the moment where I woke up in the hospital—the turning point where the people closest to me rallied around and forced me to get the help I needed.

But it was real life. And I'd grown so good at compartmentalizing my pain that I woke up, brushed my teeth, got dressed, and went to the studio. I told no one what I'd done the night before. My trust was so battered that I couldn't risk it somehow getting spread online.

The day passed like any other, but I understood that now, this was the lowest I could possibly get. That night I came home to my empty apartment and sat with myself for a long time. I didn't know what I was supposed to do. I needed to acknowledge—at least to myself—what had happened the night before.

I could visualize a crossroads clearly in my head. This wasn't a point I could turn back from. Either I would fix this, fix *everything*, or at least try to, or I would end up losing this battle with myself very soon. This limbo I was in wasn't sustainable.

I wish I could say it was an easy choice, but it wasn't. I had to ask myself: Do you really want to die, or do you just want to be somewhere else? Somewhere kinder?

Or, if I was given a magic wand that could fix all the pain, would I still want to be gone?

The answer was no.

I started there, with the realization that my life wasn't irredeemable. I tried to let it be that simple: I chose to live, even just one day more. I knew that meant putting in work, that I had to start showing up for myself so I wouldn't end up regretting my decision. Because the last thing I wanted was to look back on that night and wish I had been successful in my attempt.

At first I didn't know where to start. I made this decision—this promise to myself—but there's no step-by-step guide to getting better. I didn't want to die, but now I needed to figure out how to turn my life into one I wanted to live.

10

Work in Progress

When I first started looking into therapy, I was reluctant and skeptical. I'd gone to a few different therapists before, but nothing truly stuck. I was at such a crisis point, though, I didn't know where else to start. I made a promise to myself to *try*, and this felt like the only logical first step.

Today I believe that everyone, in all walks of life, no matter how "perfect" they think they are, can benefit from therapy. But for a long time I vehemently resisted it. It felt like a cop-out. It was always the first thing suggested to me whenever I opened up about how I was struggling.

"Are you in therapy?" they'd ask, as if it was that easy, as if I could be shipped off to some professional so no one else would have to worry about me. But I was convinced I already knew everything that was wrong with me; I didn't need someone else to point it out.

Though I wouldn't admit it at the time, there was also another part of me that—despite myself—didn't want to get better. I was at such a low that I convinced myself that happiness was an intangible concept—that everyone who claimed to be truly happy was lying. I thought everyone went around life faking a smile the same way I did. I told myself that I was just smart enough to see the world for what it was, that my veil had been lifted at a young age and I was just more in touch with reality.

But really, thinking that way was a trap that kept me buried six feet under. Even at my lowest, with no way to go but up, I was still working against myself. I operated out of fear.

There were so many people in my life who would be ready and willing to help, but they were on standby until I decided I wanted it for myself.

For a long time I buried a lot of things that I never wanted to discuss, or even *acknowledge* might have happened to me. Even now, there are still things that have happened to me that I struggle to talk about—let alone write about—and when I finally started therapy, they were even more tucked away. Going to therapy meant facing those imperfect parts of myself, digging up pieces of my past that I would have rather kept buried. It was a hard decision, but one of the best ones I've ever made.

But broaching the subject of trauma with my therapist was confusing and disorienting.

"Well, when you're dealing with trauma of this nature . . . ," she started, but the look on my face was enough to stop her.

"With what?" I laughed under my breath. "I don't have PTSD."

"What makes you think that?" she asked, so sincere that I had to pause and think.

"It sounds a little extreme, is all."

"It's post-traumatic stress, Madison," she reminded me. "Was everything you've dealt with—all we've discussed—not traumatic for you?"

"*Traumatic* is a big word."

"Trauma is distress without resolution," she explained. "Did, let's say, having your privacy violated at fifteen cause you distress?"

I nodded slowly.

"And do you still live with the effects of it?"

I nodded.

"So it's not fully resolved."

I sighed. "Okay, but that's nothing compared to what other people go through."

"If you had a broken wrist, would you stop yourself from going to the hospital because someone in Ohio had a broken leg?"

Frowning, I shook my head.

"So different types of pain can all exist at once. It's not a competition of who has it worse. And someone else's pain doesn't take away from your own."

I remained silent. In my head, I was already imagining the comments online if I were to even hint at having trauma. I thought I'd be torn apart.

"You have to acknowledge that the wound is there before you can take the steps to heal it," she told me. I sank back in my chair. Deep down, I knew she was right, but I'd spent so much time denying that trauma that having to face it head-on was daunting.

I wrote one of my favorite songs during this point in my life. In the first verse of "Effortlessly," I sing, "Here's a little pill, here's a little fix-it-all," about my first experiences with being medicated for my depression.

My introduction to medication was rocky at best. Given that I was suicidal, the goal was to get me on something to help stabilize me, to keep me safe enough for the time being, so I could focus on therapy and address some of the underlying issues.

But after a point, after hopping back and forth between different medications and experiencing no significant changes, I grew less and less hopeful that there was some sort of "magic pill" that would fix me. And soon it began to feel like the focus was more on finding a medication that would keep me from harming myself than on eliminating the reasons I wanted to harm myself in the first place.

As mentioned earlier, I was extremely addicted to Xanax. A friend had given me a bar at a sleepover after a night of running around LA. I was instantly hooked. I loved the strange numbness, a slight detachment from the world.

I kept that a secret. This dependency was only growing, and it wasn't something I was proud of. Instead of helping me regulate my emotions, Xanax kept me too numb. I became completely addicted to it and began majorly abusing it. I lost my appetite, slept constantly, and struggled to focus, but I believed it was better than being able to feel all the raw pain of my lowest points. I wasn't experiencing the true extent of happiness, either, but I was at such a low that I didn't care. I wanted to be numb. I'd sacrifice true happiness if it meant avoiding true sadness.

Don't get me wrong—medicine, even Xanax in many cases, is great and helpful and truly does work. I have so many friends whose lives have been saved because of it. But for me, the Xanax did the opposite of what it was supposed to. I went to therapy less and less because I thought the medicine would be enough. It wasn't working with me, it was working against me. I used it as a crutch—using the side effects as a Band-Aid over a wound much deeper. I told my psychiatrist and my therapist that I felt better, but the people around me started to notice just how different I was acting.

"What's up with you?"

I frowned at my brother. I'd invited him and his friends over to my apartment, but I was regretting it already. They were loud and rowdy and overwhelming. It was still early in the day, but I already wanted to crawl back into bed, put on a movie, and sleep.

"You're acting weird." He looked at me, narrowing his eyes, and I shrank back into my place on the couch, as if he was somehow reading my mind. "Are you on drugs?"

"No." I scoffed, rolling my eyes. "God, no. I'm just tired."

"No, Mad, I'm serious." He shook his head. "It's not just today. It's, like, all the fucking time now. It's like the thing that makes you Madison is gone. Like you're a zombie."

I tensed. Hearing that from one of the most important people in my life was like a punch in the gut. We'd grown up together. If there's one person who's known me at every single stage of my life, every high and low—it's him. And he was right.

I was numbed—sluggish and tired all the time. I knew it all already, that my reliance on Xanax was getting out of control, that I needed to ask for help, but I was so terrified of losing that buffer between me and the world.

With Xanax, it was so much easier to detach from myself—to

stay numb and focus on surviving day by day. But that wasn't the goal of being medicated. I wasn't experiencing life the way I should have been. And if that was affecting someone as important to me as my little brother, I couldn't lie to myself and pretend I was fine anymore.

Yes, the right medication could help me better navigate my issues, but no pill I could take would do the self-work I needed to do in therapy, reverse what I went through, or find me a stronger support system. Those were things I needed to do on my own.

Getting off Xanax was like reintroducing myself to the world. It was difficult. But something ignited a fire under me. I wish I knew what exactly changed, but maybe my motivation stemmed out of pure frustration with myself and the world around me. I wanted to get better, even if it was just out of spite. I was so fed up with feeling this way that something had to give. I was able to detox and get myself off the drug for a few months, but I relapsed time and time again. My journey with it hasn't stopped three years later. I am currently off it, but six months ago I was not.

After deciding to truly quit for the first time, my goals in therapy started shifting. Before, I had been at such a low that my only worries were surviving day-to-day—getting out of bed, getting enough food and water in my body, and getting enough sleep. But I knew I needed to do more.

If a flower doesn't grow, you don't blame the flower—you inspect what might be hindering its ability to grow. Is it getting enough sunlight? Enough water? Is it in bad soil?

As much as depression and anxiety are chemical imbalances, there are also so many outside factors that influence our mental health. I had to look at my entire life as objectively as I could and decide what wasn't working for me.

Was I overworking myself in one area of my life and neglecting myself in another? Was I surrounding myself with people that didn't have my best interests at heart? Was I staying in a friendship or relationship that inhibited my growth? I even had to question if living in such a crowded area of Los Angeles was helping or hindering me. I pulled up all the roots I'd put down, just to make sure they were still serving me.

It was a slow process, but I started adjusting the staples of my life. I put distance between myself and friend groups who made me feel bad about myself—friends who I felt like I couldn't truly be myself around. I adjusted my work schedule so it worked more like a nine-to-five job, giving me the assurance that I had at least one day off a week. I realized I needed a set time to unwind that I could look forward to, instead of feeling like I had to constantly be accessible. I set healthy boundaries to keep me sane. It was a huge step in the right direction, and for the first time in a long time, I felt somewhat in control again.

It wasn't long after this that I ended up meeting my best friend, Lena.

To make a long and lovely story short, I somehow stumbled across her Instagram account, where she had a post she had written about me as part of a course she was taking for college. She described—as a stranger—how it felt to watch me grow all of these years. She spoke about my journey and how it resonated with her, and how it pertained to the bigger picture of social media and its impact on young girls.

She saw me. She really, really saw me, more clearly than I believe any person had ever seen me before. She showed true empathy for a total and utter stranger, and that wasn't something I was used to. I reached out to her after reading what she had written, and honestly, we instantly became best friends. She is such a gift.

Growing up, my friends and I didn't speak openly about mental health. And I had a circle of friends in Los Angeles, but I struggled to find true depth there, when our shared interests always seemed to revolve around going out to parties or sitting around and gossiping. I've definitely gained some incredible friends out here, but I felt alone a lot of the time.

Lena was different. As she and I got closer and I opened up more and more, she listened. And she didn't try to talk me out of what I was feeling. She cared in a way no girl my age has truly ever cared, and leveled with me in a way no one else has. From the start, I never had to translate myself to her. There was no pressure to overexplain things. We'd come from entirely different upbringings, with completely different life experiences and aspirations, but somehow, she got it.

I'd gotten more open to therapy, but it had become routine. And it had started feeling like the only person who cared—the only person who would listen—was a person paid to do so. Meeting Lena was one of the first times where I felt I had someone who cared and listened without expecting anything in return. We were friends. Actual, true friends. I was experiencing what genuine friendship and reciprocation felt like for the first time in what seemed like forever. It was new for me, especially after being hurt by so many people in the past.

I spent so much time believing that everyone was out to get me, that everyone in my life was going to screw me over eventually. But having a best friend who showed up for me, who cared for me, who saw the good in me even when I couldn't see it for myself, made me feel so much less alone.

I bring this up because I want to emphasize how much having a true and loving friend in this world can help or change someone's life. It changed mine. *She* changed mine. I always say that Lena is my true guardian angel. I've never had someone love me for me in the ways she does.

In life, we usually prioritize our romantic relationships so much more than our platonic ones. We have a laundry list of what we would require from a lover, but not a friend. Lena broke all the regulations I had ever had about making a friend. She changed what love means in my eyes—what true friendship is. She was a light in the dark for me. Our friendship blossomed, and continues to. The first time we met in person after talking nonstop for well over a year was the most delightfully wholesome experience. We had gone to the deepest corners of each other's souls in conversation, staying up all hours of the night on FaceTime, but honestly, I had no idea what her favorite type of pasta was. We sat across from each other at lunch for the first time and couldn't help but laugh at our attempts to make small talk.

Lena's importance and impact on my life are undeniable, and this book is a perfect example of how intertwined our souls really are. I'd always wanted to be more open about my journey, but I never knew how to even begin going about it. I felt frightened and alone, unsure if my story was even one worth sharing. Lena's affirmation and support have pushed me here. After she graduated from college with her master's degree in writing, it felt like the perfect opportunity to start entertaining the idea of actually creating this book. There is no one on the planet I would be able to trust to help me write this other than her. No one I could call and say, "Hey, I wrote this, do you think it's missing anything?" and get a response that holds so much value in my heart. A response that I trust through and through.

She is half of my heart and the other side of my brain. Meeting her and bringing her into my life made me happy my attempt hadn't been successful—as did so many things, once I started allowing myself to believe good things could happen for me again.

All this to say, there are people out there who *will* love you for you, and there are people out there who want to.

In the end, even with the external factors that started working for me, everything still boiled down to the choice I made on the night after my attempt.

My recovery wasn't overnight. And it wasn't a one-size-fits-all fix. Sometimes when I speak or write about my journey, I feel like it comes across as something that's finished. So please, don't get me wrong—I didn't skyrocket from rock bottom to cloud nine. But I pulled myself up from my low point and planted my feet on solid ground again, and seeing that growth actually *was* possible—not just a myth—made me motivated to keep pushing. And once I knew what rock bottom felt like, I wanted every precaution in place to ensure I would never wind up there again.

But just because I was more aware of the things I was dealing with, that didn't mean I was automatically healed. At the time, I thought that because I was putting work in, I was ensuring

I would never go back to that low point. So when I had a bad day—or even a bad week—I was terrified that I was slipping back into a dark place I couldn't get out of.

But that isn't how it works. It took me a while to realize "getting better" isn't about preventing myself from ever encountering negative emotions. It's about building my toolkit and having practices in place so that I can handle the lows better; it's about understanding that experiencing those bad days doesn't mean I'm reverting or losing progress, but simply that I'm human. It's all a balance. Healing isn't linear.

I'm a work in progress, and I always will be. Every day I have to wake up and make the conscious decision to keep working on myself. I have to locate patterns and habits that my brain once picked up to help me survive that don't apply to my life anymore.

At my lowest, I wasted a lot of time feeling sorry for myself, convinced that my misery was the hardest thing I would ever go through. But it was actually my journey to find healing that was the hardest—I had to start by believing I was even worthy of feelings like happiness and joy in the first place.

A Letter to Self

In a year from now, where do you want to be? What will you wish you had started doing today?

Now, write a letter to yourself as you were a year ago. How have you grown since? Tiny victories are still victories. What have you learned? What have you overcome?

Dear Madison,

As a fan of yours for a long time, after having your private videos leaked, I know having your trust betrayed has unfortunately become a common theme in your life. In what ways have you healed this part of yourself and how do you cope with it all now?

Gracie, Montana

In hindsight, having my nudes leaked was the catalyst that started my journey of self-love. Now, I don't focus on the fact that I've had my trust broken over and over—I think of it more as a lot of harsh lessons that were all blessings in disguise.

But learning how to heal from what happened meant having to even acknowledge that it happened to me in the first place. For a long time I just tried my best to move on and leave it in the past. But no matter how much I tried to pretend it didn't exist, the video continued to haunt me. My phone would buzz in the middle of the night, and even years later, I would begin to tremble. The chance that it would all happen again held me hostage in my own mind.

It wasn't a one-and-done incident. After the dust settled, I didn't get to just move on and say, "Phew, thank goodness it's over." I knew I had sent more videos to that one person than what was leaked. If this was out there, I always knew there had to be more.

One day my nightmare began to unfold right in front of me. I got an anonymous text—a single picture of a desktop computer with hundreds of files, all pixelated videos of me, giving me some sort of ultimatum if I wanted to prevent their release. We traced it back to another boy who I'd gone to school with and shut it down, but I wasn't stupid. I knew (and know, to this day) that if someone had the videos then, they still have them now. That thought always lingered in the back of my head.

It bled into every aspect of my life. My close friendships suffered. I questioned everyone in my circle, putting distance between myself and everyone around me out of fear. And making new friends was impossible when all I could think of was whether they'd seen the video or not, and whether they were somehow trying to befriend me just to expose another part of my life online.

It was the tipping point for paranoia that I still deal with to this day. It shattered any sense of privacy I felt, and for the next few years, anytime I went out in public, I was terrified that people were recording me. If I went to parties with my friends, I wouldn't dare hold a plastic cup, scared someone would take a picture and post it online and say I was drinking, and I'd be torn apart by the same people who attacked me over the video. I have so much sympathy for my younger self. If only she knew it didn't matter what people had to say. It sounds silly now to hear that my sixteen-year-old self would've rather died than be caught drinking alcohol at a party, even though most teens do anyway. If missing out on all "normal" childhood things wasn't enough, having all these other normal teenage experiences robbed from me due to paranoia was so unfair.

Even now, when I'm sitting in my backyard or swimming in my pool, I'll hear a distant noise and instantly tense up, thinking it's the shutter of a camera. To this day, hearing my phone ring in the middle of the night can trigger an anxiety attack, and my heart picks up speed the exact same way it did the night that the videos were leaked.

It wasn't until years and years passed that I finally believed that maybe, *hopefully*, the video was in the past. But then, on the morning of my twenty-first birthday, I woke up to a phone call from my current manager.

I sat there listening to her try and explain (as carefully as she could) that the video had started resurfacing online. In an instant I was fifteen years old again, and all the time I'd spent trying to deny it had ever happened to me vanished. It'd been almost six years, and I'd yet to truly acknowledge that it had happened to me.

My manager was mid-apology, telling me my team was going to take care of it, but I was hardly listening to her anymore. Even if the videos were removed before they blew up on social media again, they'd still be haunting me for the rest of my life.

I sat there and stared at the mirror for a long time after we hung up. I felt sick. But at that moment—all those years later—it finally clicked for me.

I found a photo of myself when I was fifteen and looked at it for a long time, until the girl in the photo was unrecognizable. I was a *child*. It hit me just how young I was when I went through this, and I finally realized that I was the true victim in that situation, and that I was even *allowed* to be a victim in the first place.

Then, as I looked back, it was easier to understand that I

didn't do anything wrong, aside from trusting the wrong person. But at the time—when I was the one going through it—everyone around me made me feel like I made such an adult mistake, that the responsibility fell on my shoulders and my shoulders only. I wasn't allowed to be upset, because I had ultimately brought it upon myself.

Never mind the person who leaked the video in the first place. Never mind the boys in my hometown who posted it online, the thousands of users online who spread around an explicit video of an underage girl, or the news outlets that drew more attention to it—no. None of them got in trouble.

Because I had taken the video in the first place—even if I only sent it to someone I had known for years, through an app that was private, with the confidence that I could trust him—I was told things as extreme as that I deserved to die. And at twenty-one, I realized just how ridiculous that was.

That was the biggest hurdle I had to jump over in order to start healing—first, I had to forgive myself.

But now, I was angry. I couldn't let myself be that scared fifteen-year-old girl again, and I sure wasn't going to let the people circulating that video believe that it was something worth shaming me for. I had a duty to protect the girl I once was. I called my manager back.

"I'm going to write something about this and post it on my Instagram," I told her, not bothering to ask for permission. "This time, I want to get them before they can get me."

On International Women's Day 2020, I posted a statement on my Instagram, finally acknowledging that it had been me in the videos, and explaining why I was no longer allowing myself to be ashamed of them. Instead, I pointed the shame toward the ones who betrayed the trust of a fifteen-year-old girl. Even though it was just a single post, to this day, I consider it one of the most important decisions in my life. I needed to take back my power, no matter the consequences.

But still, I was surprised at how much courage it took to finally press POST. And what surprised me even more was how positively it was received. I wanted to take my power back, but before I posted, I also had to accept that my career or reputation might take a hit. I had to make sure I was ready to handle whatever hate I'd get, because my experience at fifteen had conditioned me into thinking that this was something I deserved to be hated for.

But that didn't happen. Instead, I got apologies from some of the people who had spread the video all those years ago. Young girls who had their trust betrayed in similar ways reached out to me, thanking me for making them feel less alone.

I should have been thanking them, too, because their responses were invaluable in my healing. And I wished I could have gone back and shown these messages to my fifteen-year-old self—to make *her* feel less alone, too, and to prove to her that she wasn't the only person going through this.

Here's the thing—I should have been better protected. It's a federal crime to knowingly send or receive any image of a minor engaging in sexually explicit conduct. Yes, I had sent the video in the first place, but there were also hundreds—if not thousands—of other people who sent and received it. And I wasn't the one who distributed it online.

Over the years there have been countless stories of young

girls who have had their trust betrayed in the exact same way, while all the adults around them choose to sweep things under the rug instead of pursuing justice. In 2016 a fifteen-year-old girl killed herself after her ex-boyfriend posted a nude video of her to Twitter—and her story is one of many. Yet to this day no federal laws revolve around revenge porn.

For my own good, I try not to spend too much time reflecting on all the ways my situation could have been better handled, but when I do, I'm just left feeling gutted for that fifteen-year-old girl I was, who didn't even realize she was a victim. Who thought she was disgusting for exploring her body and sexuality in a way most teenagers do. Who was taught to hate herself and her body because of someone else's selfish choices.

It's been almost a decade now since that incident, and even though the internet can still be brutal, I am hopeful that something like this wouldn't happen today. The internet was a different place back then. People had a lot more anonymity, and the law was still struggling to figure out how to deal with crimes happening online. The words *sexting* and *cyberbullying* weren't even added to the *Oxford English Dictionary* until 2011.[*]

I hope now, if the same thing were to happen to another fifteen-year-old, social media platforms would be forced to take more responsibility to stop the distribution of the materials. We have more of an understanding of how damaging (not to mention

---

[*] Chenda Ngak, "Retweet, Sexting and Cyberbullying Added to Oxford English Dictionary," CBS News (CBS Interactive, August 29, 2011), https://www.cbsnews.com/news/retweet-sexting-and-cyberbullying-added-to-oxford-english-dictionary/.

illegal) something like this is. But I also think the culture on-line has changed, and that we've become a lot more self-policing, enough that online communities would rally around the victim and work to stop explicit content of a minor from being spread further. I have to believe we would do better.

But most importantly, I am no longer ashamed. Realizing that was the first step.

11

The Road Not Taken

During my journey with therapy and medication, I was thrown a handful of different diagnoses. Multiple doctors tried to put a label on me after only one session. One simply told me, "Well, I guess you could be schizophrenic," and sent me on my way. I was discouraged, confused, and overwhelmed with information. It made me feel even worse. Was I so far beyond repair that even a professional couldn't figure out what was wrong with me?

However, BPD and OCD were the only diagnoses I received from multiple doctors, and they were the first diagnoses that—when I began doing my research—felt like the answer I'd been searching for.

Borderline personality disorder (BPD) is defined by the National Alliance on Mental Illness as a "condition characterized by difficulties regulating emotion. This means that people who experience BPD feel emotions intensely and for extended periods, and it is harder for them to return to a stable baseline after an emotionally triggering event.'"

When I was first diagnosed, my initial relief was followed by a slew of mixed emotions. On the one hand, it was nice to have confirmation that I wasn't "crazy." I'd harbored so much guilt for years, always believing I was my own worst enemy. Why did I torture myself? Why did I always seem to seek out the things that upset me? Putting a name to it was affirming.

On the other hand, I went through a period of grieving. The diagnosis initially felt like some sort of life sentence—a flaw in my code without any cure. How had I gotten here? Had I done something to bring this upon myself? Would I have to struggle with it for the rest of my life? I would get angry when I thought back to all the people in my life—in my childhood—who could've been responsible for doing this to me. I felt like I'd been robbed of the chance to live a "normal" life, long before I even posted my first YouTube video.

There are also times when I can't help but wonder if I'd still have BPD if I hadn't stuck with my career. When I look at the symptoms on paper, it's almost laughable, as if they're all side effects of "fame," and everything that comes along with it.

- **Extreme fear of abandonment** from being dropped by my first label, and from gaining and losing friends so often in my teenage years.

"Borderline Personality Disorder," NAMI California, April 21, 2020, https://namica.org/illnesses/borderline-personality-disorder/.

- **Restless and rapidly changing self-image** from being exposed to other people's opinions of me before I developed true opinions about myself.
- **Recurring suicidal patterns** from being put in situations where it felt like the world was against me, making me believe the only way out was through ending my life entirely.
- **Feelings of paranoia and isolation** from having my trust betrayed over and over, from feeling like I had no one else who understood what I was going through because my experience was unique.

The list goes on. It feels like my entire life's journey thus far has been a perfectly crafted cocktail of situations that landed me at this diagnosis, as if my biography could be written and titled *How to Give Someone BPD: A Step-by-Step Guide.*

When it comes to personality disorders, everyone experiences different symptoms in different severities, so my experience with BPD is very personal. When I speak about it, I'm speaking about my experience alone, not the experience of the community as a whole.

There's a lot of mental pain and anguish that comes with BPD. It's hard for me to feel comfortable and stable when I'm in a happy mood, because my knee-jerk reaction is to anticipate the impending crash. And when I'm upset, the emotions are so strong and consuming that it's difficult for me to remember that they won't last forever. It's hard for me to exist between those extremes.

But because it's rarely talked about, BPD is easily stigmatized and looked down upon. From the outside, people see intense emotions and write them off as overreacting. But when I'm in a bad headspace and someone tells me, "It's not the end of the world," it comes across as an insult. Even if you can't feel the pain for yourself, even if you don't think you'd feel the same in my position, the pain is real to me.

I feel a lot. And I feel things deeply. I value those things about myself. I have a lot of passion and a lot of empathy for the people around me. As I learn how to better cope with the ups and downs of my emotions, I also try to be mindful of the ways my BPD makes me unique.

It makes me a better artist. I can convey emotion through my lyrics and singing. I can easily tap back into my pain and turn it into art—which I think is one of the most beautiful things we can do to grow. It's not a life sentence like I thought it was. I'm not doomed to suffer forever, and I embrace the things it's taught me.

I kept my BPD diagnosis to myself for a while. At the start, I figured it was something I should handle in private. I didn't feel ready to talk about it. But over time it began to feel like I was keeping it hidden, as if it was something to be ashamed of, and I didn't like the message that would be sending. I knew so many of my fans struggled in similar ways, and *not* sharing my story felt like a wasted opportunity. I googled "celebrities with BPD" and only a handful of men came up. I didn't see it represented anywhere, especially in young females. I wanted to be an advocate in a space that was otherwise pretty empty.

In 2020, I slowly started talking more publicly about my journey with mental health, including my BPD diagnosis. I thought it would be much scarier than it actually was. Instead, it felt like

I was aching to get it out. Getting diagnosed helped me feel less alone, and all I wanted to do was extend that same comfort to other people who might be in the same boat as me.

In August of that year, when I was officially one year clean, I opened up about my struggle with self-harm. In some ways, that was even more difficult than opening up about the leaking of my nudes. More people wanted to contest it. But the support and solidarity I received far outweighed those trying to discredit me. Once I tied this in with my BPD advocacy, I became more and more confident about sharing my story.

I started being invited to discuss those topics in my interviews, and I found I really enjoyed being able to talk about something that I felt so strongly about. I felt I made more of a difference in the lives of my fans when I was being real and honest about our shared points of struggle, instead of answering surface-level or repetitive questions.

I've always had a strong connection with my fans, but this forged an even deeper bond. Often I get messages from my fans telling me how much I've helped them; a handful of them tell me that I saved their lives, or influenced them to stop self-harming, start going to therapy, and take their mental health seriously.

It's the biggest honor in the world, and it makes me feel like I'm doing something worthwhile with the platform I've been given, but I'm also adamant about reminding them that at the end of the day, *they* showed up for themselves. They saved their own lives, in the same way I had all the resources in the world at my disposal, but my healing only came when I was the one in the driver's seat.

What my fans didn't realize was that it was just as healing

for me as it was for them. Slowly, I was stitching up that split between my true self and the "Madison Beer" I put on for the public. Being able to turn my pain into something that could help others was integral to my own healing. It gave me an even stronger sense of purpose. I felt like I was finally allowing myself to be seen as human without a debilitating fear of being judged for it.

The promise I made to myself—to stay alive—was now growing into something bigger. I was doing it for myself, but I was also now staying alive to prove a point to all the young adults who looked up to me. I thought I would have to be fully healed and "move on" before I ever approached the idea of talking about it publicly, but I think it makes more of a difference when I tell my fans, "Hey, I'm still struggling, too, and I still struggle every day. But we're in this together." I wouldn't hesitate to go through it all again if it meant being able to have the perspective I have now. If I can help one person feel less alone, that's all I can ask.

Dear Madison,

I finally worked up the courage to tell my parents about my struggles with self-harm, and they didn't understand at all. They think I'm just a dramatic teenager looking for attention. Am I really just overreacting?

Lily, Michigan

I still can't wrap my head around why we view mental health as something secondary to physical health, when it's just as (if not more) important. Mental health affects our physical health—the two can't be separated. We have to be in a stable headspace to make healthy decisions for our bodies. And you can't enjoy the benefits of having a healthy diet and active lifestyle if you're still miserable in your brain all day.

You wouldn't tell someone with a broken leg to "just walk it off," so why isn't that same understanding extended to mental illness? Why is someone with depression called "lazy" when they're struggling to find the motivation to get up and face the world? Why do we tell someone with anxiety that they're "overreacting" when they struggle with the idea of leaving the house?

And when it comes to self-harm, I think the reason it's become an issue specifically within my generation is because we've neglected to emphasize the importance of mental health.

A lot of people hold the view that self-harming is an attention-seeking behavior, and it's presented in a way that tries to turn it against the person suffering. I've always found that strange, because it's an argument that falls apart instantly. When I was struggling with self-harming, what attention was I seeking? I certainly wasn't looking to be praised for what I was doing, so what was I seeking? Help? Recognition of my suffering?

Because no one seemed to take my mental health seriously, I felt pushed to translate it into something visible, for the sole reason that we place greater emphasis on physical pain. And I had to prove it to myself, too. Like I needed to be a witness to my own pain, to see that it was real—that it wasn't all in my head.

In the midst of my self-harming, when people around me got wind of what was happening, they all seemed to realize: Oh, wow, this is worse than we thought. It was a big catalyst for getting me the help I needed. But I remembered how no one took action when my suffering was only mental. I only wish that we would try to be better at taking the mental health of young adults seriously before they have to reach a crisis point—before they feel the need to do something so drastic in order for their pain to be believed.

In the same way I say that when a flower doesn't grow, we don't blame the flower but rather look to its surroundings, I believe that there are bigger factors at play when it comes to my generation's struggle with mental illness. I don't think it's a coincidence that the number of teenagers dealing with depression and anxiety continues to increase.[*] Or that eating disorders are becoming more and more normalized among younger and younger children. Countless external pressures are placed on young adults—whether it's through societal standards or social media specifically—and it can be suffocating. There's a clear connection between the increase in mental illness and the way our world is changing. If we don't change the way we speak about the issue, it will only continue to get worse. That's why the least I can do is talk openly about it. Making people understand there's a problem is the first step in rallying behind a solution.

In short, no—you're not overreacting when you feel the way you do. It's a really tough world to grow up in right now. Never before have we had this much access to this much information at once. And sometimes it's difficult for parents to understand; the divide is just so great between the world they navigated as teenagers and the world as it is now.

Obviously I'm not a licensed therapist, and I'm still learning myself, but what I can tell you is what I tell myself when I'm struggling: Don't work against your body.

We're living in a world that's constantly in flux, and a lot of us feel scared of the future. But I try to make that all the more reason to look after myself. With so many things working against me and my body, I can't afford to let myself be one of them.

---

[*] "Children's Hospitals Admissions for Suicidal Thoughts, Actions Double During Past Decade," AAP News, May 4, 2017, https://publications.aap.org/aapnews/news/8333.

Getting Out of Your Way

What are some of the ways you work against yourself? What are some of the things you think you'd be able to accomplish if you didn't stand in your own way? What healthy coping mechanisms, even if they are small, can you turn to instead?

Dear Madison,

Do you ever get overwhelmed with putting yourself out there? Are there times when you wish you could put everything on pause?

Sophie, New York

To answer your question briefly, yes. There are times I do wish I could pause it all. Never be recognized, looked at, or watched. Sometimes I feel overwhelmed by the fact that there is no way out. Even if I deleted all of my social media, people out there would still talk about me, speculate about me, and perceive me. It can feel like you're trapped. I made a life-altering decision to be in the public eye at age twelve. As an adult, I do question what choices I would make differently today if I got the chance to start over.

My paranoia is one of my biggest daily struggles. More often than not, I feel like I'm under constant surveillance.

At the end of the day, I don't think humans were ever meant to be this visible. I don't think our brains can even process the true size and reach of the internet. Currently, my most viewed music video has forty-two million views. Never in my life will I set foot in a room with a million people, let alone forty-two million. I can't even begin to fathom that many pairs of eyes on me.

We tend to forget just how new the idea of social media is. Our generation has always straddled the fence between old technology and new technology. We're the last generation that will remember what the world was like before social media. Now, kids are practically born holding iPads, but I still remember how mind-blown I was by my mom's chunky flip phone.

I remember the fall of Myspace and the rise of Facebook, but a majority of my audience has never known a world without social media. In the grand scheme of things—in the timeline of our society in particular—it's still in its infancy. The World Wide Web was invented in 1989—thirty-four years before the publication of this book. The idea of social media didn't even exist until 1997, twenty-six years before the publication of this book.

Instagram was launched in 2010, and its impact is continuing to evolve. At first it acted as a simple photo sharing and editing app, but now there are users whose presence on Instagram is their full-time job. My career relies on social media. If the internet were to mysteriously vanish tomorrow, I'd have no way to connect directly with my fans. It's so fragile and superficial, and yet my "job" relies on it. It's a concept I still grapple with.

Having my name out there so young kick-started a lot of my fear revolving around being so open for public consumption, but as I slowly started making a name for myself after going independent, I found myself in the spotlight more and more, and that paranoia was only exacerbated. I had no choice but to get used to it. It was never not on my mind. It's scary enough learning to drive as a teenager in Los Angeles, but when I started, I was always on edge, keeping an eye out for any suspicious-looking cars that followed me for too long, always circling the block a few times to make sure I wasn't being followed back to my apartment.

When I was going through a public breakup, I was terrified of leaving my building. My friends would invite me out to try and get my mind off things, and I'd decline simply because I was so afraid of running into someone—whether it be a fan or paparazzi—and being cornered with questions about my ex. (If I wasn't "famous," and someone with a camera was following me—a lone female—around the city by themselves, wouldn't that raise suspicion? When does it cross a line?)

From the outside, it seemed like the world was at my feet. I was eighteen and single and living on my own in one of the busiest cities in the world. But really I'd never felt more trapped, scared to leave my apartment and confront the world face-to-face.

There's also a big difference between the times that I'm aware I'm being "consumed" and the times when I'm not. In a handful of instances, people have posted videos of me in public when I had no idea I was being filmed. Even if it's only happened a few times, it's jarring, and now I'm forced to operate under the assumption that whenever I'm in public, even if I think the coast is clear, I'm always being watched.

I've had people I considered friends take sneaky pictures of me when they thought I wasn't looking. I once had a therapist disclose private information about me to their other clients. Sometimes when I meet people, they'll have their phones hidden, trying to be discreet, but I always know when I'm being secretly recorded, even if the person is pretending not to know who I am. In those cases, I know it's not done with bad intentions, but it still puts me in an odd position.

In short, people I've trusted have, over and over, betrayed that trust. And the more it happened, the more it started to alter the way I went about daily life. I'm not exaggerating when I say it rewires your brain and thought patterns. I find myself worrying over the smallest things. I anticipate every way something can go wrong—every possible fault someone could comment on. My brain gets trapped on a thought, and I spiral quickly.

If I'm in a hurry at the grocery store and don't make small talk with the cashier, I'll drive away scared that they know who I am, that they'll go online and post, "Wow, Madison Beer just came into my store and didn't even look at me, she thinks she's better than everyone."

If I have a friend over and we're talking about something personal, a small, nagging voice in the back of my head always makes me wonder if they're recording me, or keeping screenshots of our text conversations, and whether they'll post them online at the slightest provocation as some sort of "exposé" on me.

When I'm staying in hotel rooms on tour, I can't go to bed until I sweep the room for cameras or microphones. Once, when I was on tour, I had my dog's leash in one hand and a suitcase in the other, and I had to open the door with my hip and then kick it open with the ball of my foot. The kick was more forceful than I anticipated, and the door slammed back against the wall. When I thought about it again later that night, I couldn't sleep. Somehow I wound up convincing myself that someone had heard the bang, checked the security cameras, gotten that footage of me, and would post it online and try to make it seem like I had a tantrum and kicked down a door. This is the constant state I function in.

It sounds ridiculous when I write it out, I know. But it affects me all the same. There are very few times where I feel completely unseen. There's only a handful of people I feel secure with, and an even smaller select few who I can say I trust wholeheartedly.

Even if it were all to go away tomorrow, I would still be left with a million other people's voices circulating in my head. Truthfully, it makes me feel horribly self-centered, but it stems out of a place of self-preservation. Unfortunately, there have been so many times that my paranoia was proven *right* that it's hard to write off those worries as irrational. Even in writing this book, I keep trying to censor myself, anticipating every possible criticism I might face for the way I handle certain things, the advice I give, or the stories I choose to share. It isn't human to be on twenty-four seven, for anyone. But years and years of being made fun of for the smallest things change you as a person. Trending on Twitter for over twenty-four hours straight, with over two hundred thousand tweets under a hashtag saying you are "over," is horrible. It's something I don't wish upon my worst enemy. I have grown leaps and bounds when it comes to freeing myself from online opinion, but when it feels like a tsunami of hate surrounds your name, it can be hard to ignore. I am proud of my progress, and I will continue to be myself and live a pure-intentioned life. If I put pressure on myself to be perfect all the time—whatever that means—I am not doing anyone any favors. I don't want people to like or love someone I am not, and I don't want to live an inauthentic life. Taking a step back and being present has changed so much for me. (Hence writing this book.)

That lack of trust affects my close relationships; I'm always questioning the intentions of people around me. It takes a long time for me to make new friends, and when I do, it takes even longer for me to feel comfortable opening up to them fully. And there are times when I worry about coming across as obsessive. If I call a friend and ask for their perspective on something—

whether it be the way I answered a question in an interview, or how I handled a paparazzo who approached me—I feel like I'm annoying them by asking for reassurance they've already given me countless times before.

Realistically, as long as I choose to stay public, I will always be acutely aware of the eyes on me. I understand that, and I've made peace with it. I wouldn't sacrifice the things I have now to get rid of it, but there are moments where I'm reminded of its potential to truly interfere with my life. It's a balancing act that can easily overwhelm me.

In the summer of 2021, I was working nonstop. I had meetings in the morning, studio sessions almost every day, and even in bed I was glued to my phone, to my countless work group chats, trying to keep up with an ever-changing schedule that was starting to slip from my control.

On one night in particular, all of the running around started catching up to me. I wish I could remember it better. All I know is that it felt like I was pushing off a panic attack all day, feeling a weird tightness in my chest, a fog in my brain. I had work to get done, and I powered through it, but once I pulled into the driveway, well past midnight, and set foot inside my house, I felt like everything was closing in on me.

I just wanted to sleep. That was the only thought running through my head. I just wanted to sleep and be free of the anxiety, the way my body felt like it could never truly relax, my thoughts spinning a million miles an hour. I wanted it all to stop, and the more it went on, the less I cared about the lengths I would have to go to.

I don't think I was trying to kill myself. I didn't want to die. I'd been in that place before, and this wasn't it. I really, truly just wanted to sleep. I wanted a break. The details are blurry, but I dug through my drawers in my bedroom and collected a handful of pill bottles, lining them all up and squinting to read the names. I had a few anxiety medications on hand from old prescriptions, a handful of sleeping pills, and some odd allergy medications. I don't know which ones I took, or if I took a mixture of them; I just know I took four pills that I thought would help me calm down and fall asleep.

What I didn't expect was how fast they would take effect. I went downstairs to get a glass of water, and by the time I was climbing back upstairs, the world felt a little wonky, as if everything was slightly tilted. And I was winded. I stopped for a moment and pressed my palm against the wall, giving my body a chance to right itself, but something felt wrong.

I'd taken sleeping pills before. I knew how they felt in my body, how the drowsiness sank in gradually. But this was a different feeling. I took a second to right myself before climbing the stairs. My boyfriend was spending the night, and I didn't tell him what I'd done. I just smiled weakly at him and climbed into bed.

I don't know what exactly happened—if I took a combination of pills that reacted negatively with each other, or if I just took a dosage of an anxiety medication that was too high. I leaned back against the headboard and tried to focus my gaze on the ceiling. The lines of paneling were swimming in my vision like heat waves, and a heaviness settled over my chest. It felt like I'd swallowed a brick, like my body was being dragged into sleep, my heartbeat pulsing in my ears.

"I feel like I'm having a panic attack," I spoke up suddenly.

My boyfriend sat up right away. "What?"

"I feel funny." Even my words felt heavy in my mouth. I blinked a few times to try and reset my vision, but it still sat askew. "I took pills."

"The anxiety ones?"

I shook my head. "I—I don't know." I paused. "I just wanted to sleep."

"What are you saying? What did you do?"

The panic in his voice shook me, and tears started stinging at my eyes. I pressed my palms into the mattress and pushed myself up to sit, still fighting the sleep that desperately wanted to overtake me.

I motioned weakly to the bathroom. "In there."

He got up and quickly returned with the collection of bottles in his hands, looking between me and the pills, his face paled like a ghost. "Did you—"

"No, no." I leaned forward, pressing my hands against my forehead, trying to snap myself out of it with the coldness of my hands. "I just wanted to sleep. I only took four. I don't know which ones."

"Madison . . ."

"I just wanted to sleep." It felt like the only thought running through my head. All I'd wanted to do was fall asleep, but now I was fighting against it, my eyelids heavy as I reached for my phone.

"Hey, what's up?" Lena's voice was raspy when she answered, and I could tell she'd been asleep. "Madison?"

"I . . . I took some pills," I stumbled through each word. "To sleep."

"To sleep?" The sound of her sheets rustling as she sat up echoed through the phone. "Which pills?"

"I just wanted to sleep," I repeated myself, as if that was enough of an answer.

"Okay, okay, I hear you." She was quiet for a moment, but I could practically hear her thoughts racing. "Okay. Do you need to go to the hospital? Do we need to call nine-one-one?"

Just the suggestion jolted me, like the shock of jumping into freezing cold water.

And this is what I mean when I say paranoia has rewired my brain. Because even though I was fighting sleep, even though there was a darkness creeping into the corners of my vision, all I could think about was what the headlines would be the next morning.

My thoughts spiraled quickly. What if my neighbors heard the ambulance and tipped off a news outlet? What if one of the paramedics knew who I was and leaked it to the press? What if, somehow, there was a paparazzo outside my house at that very moment, who would get pictures of me being taken to the hospital?

At the time, even with my thoughts clouded, even when my life easily could have been in danger, I was instinctively more concerned about the potential publicity than I was about my own health.

"No." I shook my head, clutching my phone and looking at my boyfriend, panic rising in my voice. "No, I only took four, it's nothing, it's fine. I'm fine."

"Were you trying to . . . ," Lena started, but trailed off, hesitant to even suggest it. "*You know . . . ?* Or were you really just trying to sleep?"

"Sleep." I paused, shivering. "But now I'm scared to."

"Okay." She took a deep breath. "Okay. I still think we should call nine-one-one."

"I don't need to go to the hospital."

"You don't have to go," she said. "But just so a paramedic can come to your house and check your vitals, or look at the pills you took to make sure . . ."

"I think we should," my boyfriend added, rubbing my back. "Just to be safe."

I squeezed my eyes shut and tucked my chin to my chest, trying to focus on my breathing. I knew they were right, but my thoughts were still circling around the worst-case scenario. My heartbeat was heavy, but slow. It took everything in me not to lie back down and give in to sleep.

"Madison . . . ," Lena said again, after a long bout of silence. "I really, like, can't let you *not* get checked out. At the very least. I can't risk you getting hurt."

"Okay." I finally relented, knowing they were right. My boyfriend took that as his cue, standing up and dialing his phone. Another wave of anxiety came over me, and it took everything in me not to burst into tears.

"Tell them it's not an emergency," I pleaded with him as the phone rang. "Tell them no sirens, please. No lights or anything. Can we give them a fake name? Is that legal?"

"It's three a.m., Mad, everyone's asleep," Lena reminded me, already knowing why I was worried. "No one's going to know. And if they somehow do, you can literally just tell them you had a bad allergic reaction to something. Or that your boyfriend passed out."

"What about the paramedics?"

"What about them?"

"What if they leak something?"

"Definitely illegal," she replied instantly, and I could hear her thumbs tapping over the phone as she googled it. "Yeah, yeah, they're covered by HIPAA. They'd lose their jobs and get in legal trouble, probably. Plus they're paramedics. In Los Angeles. They've seen ten times worse than this, you know?"

"Yeah . . ."

"They're trained to help you, Mad. It'll be good for *you* just to hear confirmation that you'll be okay."

I nodded to myself, absorbing her words and trying desperately to believe them.

When the paramedics finally got there, I couldn't hold back my tears, but I did my best to smile and be polite and apologize for taking up their time. One of them laughed at me when I asked him if he wanted a water bottle. He knelt by my bed to take my blood pressure and politely declined.

"Just let me check you out first," he told me with a soft laugh. I swallowed hard, nodding, lifting my gaze to the ceiling and noticing that my vision was slightly clearer.

"I think the worst is over," I said. "I'm still tired, but I would have fallen asleep by now if it was bad enough, right?"

He finished checking my heart rate and stood up, exchanging a look with his partner. "It's still recommended that we take you to the hospital."

My entire body tensed, the panic in my chest rising up again.

"They'd just keep you there for a few hours, just to monitor you, just to be safe until whatever you took is out of your system."

"But I only took four pills, there's no way." I tried to laugh it off, to show him how ridiculous it sounded. I looked at my boyfriend, and he was skeptical. I felt like I was in a dream. "I'm not going to die, am I?"

"If you're already feeling better, that's a good sign," the paramedic reassured me. "We can't force you to go, but we also don't know the exact pills you took. I would go, just to be safe, we usually recommend—"

"I'm not going to the hospital." I looked between him and my boyfriend. "I can't. It'll only make it worse."

"All right." The paramedic looked at his partner and nodded. "But we just need you to confirm that with the hospital, too, because they already have a bed for you. They need to hear it from you that you're refusing care and that you're liable for yourself if you don't go." It was like I was signing my life away.

He handed me a phone, and I spoke with the doctor at the hospital, listening to his obligatory warnings, answering his questions and confirming over and over again that I hadn't taken the pills with the intent to harm myself, and that I was aware of the risks of refusing treatment, and I was willing to take the risk by staying home.

The paramedics seemed reluctant as they left, but I already felt more awake, my thoughts slowly becoming more coherent. They instructed my boyfriend to wake me up every few hours to check my heart rate, and reminded me to call 911 again if I felt myself getting worse. I felt awful and selfish. I felt terrible that this was what my boyfriend had to deal with all night.

It was scary to try and fall asleep, even though I was exhausted, and it took me a while to calm down enough to even close my eyes for more than a few seconds. When I woke up in the morning, I had to piece together everything that happened the night before. I was groggy, my head aching like from a bad hangover, but I was fine physically.

Once I had a clear head, I had to sit and have a conversation with myself—another one of my crossroads moments. If I was allergic to one of the medications I took, and I hadn't gone to the hospital, I could have suffered serious side effects. Was that really a risk I wanted to take? Would I really let my own health and life come second to my paranoia? Every day I still have to reevaluate my relationship with fame and the internet, to keep myself in check and remind myself what truly matters—and it definitely isn't a news headline.

12

Glass Houses

Social media has rewired our brains. It sounds like an exaggeration, but it's true.

Since I was twelve years old, at an age when our brains are still in crucial stages of development, I was subjected to millions of unwarranted opinions about me, my body, my appearance, my personality, and my interests, which reinforced negative thought patterns that I still need years to undo. It started the day my video went viral and has not let up since.

In the early years, I tried my best to ignore the hate. Pretending it didn't exist and preaching positivity and kindness to my fans seemed like the thing I was supposed to do. Media training agreed—in interviews, it was best to turn any question about online negativity into an opportunity to gush over how grateful I was for my fans, to insist that their support was so overwhelming that it blinded me to the hate.

But it wasn't the truth. And as I got older, it felt wrong to pretend I was immune to it.

The thing is, hate doesn't get easier to deal with. Sure, I've learned to expect it. But I still read things that hurt me on a daily basis. And it's not something I, or any person, should have to get used to.

We don't understand the impact of our words. We don't realize that one sentence can completely alter the way someone feels about themselves for years to come, *especially* for young adults online. I've been hurt more by words said to me online than I have by any words spoken to me in person. The saying "Sticks and stones may break my bones but words will never hurt me" couldn't be further from the truth. Broken bones heal; words can stick with you for a lifetime.

I still have the urge to defend myself. I think it's human to want to correct someone who has a false perception of you. We all want to belong, to be accepted by our community. It's difficult for me to come to terms with the fact that there are always going to be people out there who have an image of me in their heads that's completely different from who I actually am.

Even though the online world and the real world are two very different places, it's hard to differentiate when sometimes, on an off day, we spend more time online than we do interacting with the outside world. And the pain that's caused online is very real. It's not just a matter of logging off and forgetting about it. It's not out of sight, out of mind. It sticks with you. When I look in the mirror and pick myself apart, the words in my head resemble comments I've heard since I was twelve.

It's not just a matter of kids will be kids. Unfortunately, some people don't grow out of it as they mature. I had to stop using my Facebook account when I was fifteen, after logging on to find middle-aged women saying the nastiest things about me, my body, and my personality.

Sometimes I'd indulge by clicking on their profiles and looking through their pictures, finding out that they had daughters of their own. But even worse was when I would see they were raising sons—teenage boys particularly. I can't help but wonder what kind of behavior and language toward women those boys think is acceptable if the women who raised them are comfortable with attacking a minor online. And it wasn't any better from the adult men commenting on my posts. They, too, had children. Some of them had teenage girls my age.

When I first entered this business, I expected to be treated with a lot more compassion by adults. I thought there would be a collective understanding that I was a young girl who needed protection, but some of them were just as cruel as my peers online. As I've grown older, I've realized that a lot of adults are still carrying the same wounds from their childhood. That sometimes the only thing that really changes in "growing up" is your outer appearance. But when I was young, it was a harsh reality to accept.

To this day, if I see a comment that strikes me in its severity, I'll click on the profile and take a look at the person who sent it. It helps to ground me—to put a face to a name—in the same way seeing the crowd when I performed at my ex-boyfriend's show helped to put things in perspective.

But it also hurts me to see how many seemingly normal people are so ruthlessly cruel to each other on the internet. The person who commented, "She's such a waste of space," is a normal teenage girl in the Midwest who posts pictures of her pet dog and swim team. The person who commented, "She's only tolerable when her mouth is shut," is a man in his mid-twenties whose last post was at his little sister's graduation. Over time, it becomes more and more discouraging to view humanity this way.

I tried to make sense of it for so long, but in the end it just makes me sad. It makes me want to reach out and ask them why they think it's okay to speak to someone like that. How would they feel if a person left a comment like that about someone they love? Why am I an exception?

It also makes me wonder if their close friends have any idea they're leaving these comments so openly—and if so, why aren't they holding each other accountable? Why is it acceptable? If I was ever scrolling and saw a friend of mine saying something so unnecessarily rude on someone else's post, I would have to reevaluate their place in my life. We have to hold each other to higher standards, even online.

Just because you can comment, that doesn't mean you should. Not everyone is asking for your opinion. It's a cliché, sure, but really, if you don't have anything nice to say, don't say anything at all. There's a reason this is one of the first fundamental lessons we're taught as children. I don't understand why people feel the urge to voice everything negative. It's so much easier to keep a mean thought to yourself than to waste time and energy typing out a comment.

Online, a lot of people share their personal opinions as if they're facts. And over text, it's a lot easier for someone to act like they have authority over a subject when in reality, they don't. But it should be a relief to know that you don't *have* to have an opinion on everything. You're allowed to feel neutral about people, about clothing, about controversial topics. You're allowed to dislike someone, but what's the use in vocalizing it? Investing your energy in kind comments instead—supporting creators online that you like—is so much more beneficial for everyone involved.

Sometimes the internet gives people a false sense of importance. Everyone thinks they have a platform. It's a double-edged sword. One person can make fun of you for something another person would compliment you for. I see one celebrity get praised for something another celebrity gets torn apart for. I have ten years under my belt, and I still can't predict what I'll receive hate for. There's no winning, and nothing grants anyone immunity from how cruel the internet can be.

For a while, things leveled out for me. I thought maybe the worst of it was over. That because I was older, maybe my demographic had matured along with me. Summer of 2020, I hadn't released my album yet, and I was lying pretty low. But then videos of me started going viral on TikTok. And once one video gains traction, it snowballs. On TikTok, when people see that talking about a certain topic brings in quick views, they all jump on the bandwagon.

I had enough going on in my personal life alone, and on this night in particular it was like TikTok's algorithm insisted on showing me every video that had been created about me back-to-back. TikTok's comment section can be especially brutal, and even if the video wasn't a direct hate video against me, the comments were full of users nitpicking my every move.

"Proud to say I've never liked her."
"Why does she talk like that?"

"She's so cringey."

"She's trying too hard."

"Remind me why she's famous again?"

"Who let her out of the house looking like that?"

I got more and more frustrated as I scrolled, realizing that it really was impossible to escape, even when I was sitting in bed, just trying to unwind.

At my wit's end, I called a close friend in the industry, one of the few people I know who have experienced the same level of online harassment firsthand.

"Listen, I know it sucks," she started. "Believe me, I know. But this is never going to go away."

At this point I was crying, all my stress from the past week spilling over. I expected her to try and comfort me, but the sternness in her tone took me by surprise.

"You have to figure out a way to ignore it, Madison. And if you can't—if it's going to hurt you this badly every time—maybe this isn't the career path for you. I know it's not right, but this is the kind of stuff that comes along with it. It just is."

I'd never had anyone put it that bluntly to me before. I knew what she meant, because at the end of the day, the only reaction I could control was my own. But I sat there for a while after the call ended, hating the fact that it was the truth, and that it was coming from someone who'd gone through it, too. Had she really just learned to accept it? Why did it have to be mutually exclusive?

Why was this amount of abuse something I just had to accept as part of having a platform?

Whenever someone speaks up about how the hate affects them, the backlash is always something along the lines of "Well, sorry, but you shouldn't be in this career if you can't handle it." But what about "You shouldn't be on social media if you can't conduct yourself responsibly?" What about "We need to do a better job of protecting each other online?"

If I let myself view it as normal, I would be accepting treatment I didn't deserve. It didn't feel like something I could compromise on. It was wrong. And I wanted to keep fighting against it—I had to be vocal about its effects, even just to maintain my honesty with my fans.

For me, it boiled down to one question: Who am I helping by pretending that it doesn't affect me? No one.

If anything, pretending to be above the hurt only gives haters a free pass. Either people will think it's okay to keep being abusive online because it doesn't hurt me anyway, or they'll ramp up the hate for the sole reason of seeing how much it takes to actually get through to me.

These are things no one would dare say to my face, because they'd be too afraid. It's a form of public humiliation. Sometimes I hesitate to use the word *cyberbullying* because it downplays the severity. If a partner or a family member used the same insults to me that I hear online, it would qualify as verbal abuse. Yet for some reason we don't take it seriously when it's over a computer screen. I would never tell my future child, if they're getting bullied, that they just have to suck it up and get used to it.

Even though I'm in a place where I know I'm strong enough to handle it, I shouldn't have to be. And I worry more about my other peers online, who haven't had years to get used to it.

I worry about young girls who post a video on TikTok for their close friends that accidentally goes viral, and suddenly they're drowning in hateful comments they never asked for.

I truly believe bandwagon hate online kills, in the same exact way bullying in schools is linked to teen suicide. We've lost way too many lives to hate and bullying *not* to learn our lesson as a society.

But it shouldn't take the threat of suicide to make my case. Yes, there are people who have died because of bullying, but there are also even more people who walk around every day with really deep wounds—confidence issues, depression, anxiety, eating disorders—because of something they read online and internalized.

Remember—when you post something negative about someone else's body, even if they never see it themselves, someone else with the same feature might. And you might hurt someone you never intended to hurt. A celebrity might never see your comment about their weight, but your close friends who struggle in silence will. Words are weapons that you can't unspeak.

It's unacceptable, and I hope that if I talk about it, at least a handful of people will think twice before they leave a comment that could harm someone. That's all I can ask.

Owning Up

Have you ever left a negative comment about someone? Maybe even me? If so, how do you feel about that now? If you could apologize for what you said to this person, what would you say?

If you have never left a negative comment online toward someone, but you make negative remarks toward yourself, how would you apologize to yourself? How can you practice showing not only others but also yourself the utmost empathy?

Dear Madison,

How do you tell the difference between a fake friend and a real one? How do you even find real friends in the first place?

Laila, Florida

We live in a world that puts a lot of importance on independence and individuality. Both are good qualities to have as young adults, but sometimes we skew too far in one direction. We're so busy focusing on ourselves, trying to get by day by day, that sometimes we tend to neglect the fact that we have a responsibility to uplift and look out for each other.

Humans are social creatures. Throughout history, we've always lived in close-knit communities and relied on each other for protection. Whether it's through blood family or chosen family or a mixture of both, we need each other to survive. Sometimes that's difficult to admit. I struggled the most when I thought I was supposed to do everything alone.

Even if we try to deny it, the people we keep close are a reflection of us. Their values, their morals, their views of the world, all influence and shape you, too. As I matured, I had to look at a lot of people in my life and think: You know what? I don't think I like the person I am around you.

I know cutting off friends is easier said than done, and friend breakups can be just as hard as—if not harder than—romantic ones. I believe that everyone is fighting their own battles, so maybe before just cutting all ties with someone you care about, try to work through the issue. Maybe your perspectives are different; maybe they didn't know how you were feeling. I personally believe this is the best step to seeing who even deserves your friendship in the first place. A true friend will work through it with you, or at least try. Others will not, and that is okay.

But for so long I didn't want to let go of certain people that I knew, deep down, were bad for me. I thought I could heal myself without having to change the people around me. But really, I was still putting myself in rooms with people who didn't have my best interests at heart, staying in friendships with people who never mirrored the same effort and loyalty I showed them.

I've always had a debilitating fear of the dark. It stems from a traumatic event that happened to me when I was quite young, and it's plagued me for most of my life. It's never let up, thanks to a handful of other situations that followed the first one. Somehow, the darkness continues to be involved in all of them.

I fear blackouts. Even at my concerts, the short intervals of darkness always shake me, but because I know what's coming, I manage to make it through okay. It sounds like a silly fear, I know, and I always feel embarrassed when I open up about it, but it truly is one of the most terrifying triggers for me. Everyone in my close circle is hyperaware of it. My house is outfitted with nightlights and my bedroom is never anywhere near pitch-black. When we go to amusement parks, my close friends are a step behind me—always ready with a phone flashlight if any of the attractions are too dark.

There was a time in my life when that wasn't the case. One

night when I was a teenager, a group of friends and I were playing the game called sardines, which is essentially a form of hide-and-seek in the dark. Thankfully, the home we were playing in was well lit enough, but I was still careful about sticking close to the group.

We'd gotten down to only a few people left, and there was one bedroom we hadn't checked. I was the only one brave enough to open the door, but when I did, the room was pitch-black. And suddenly I was shoved forward, everyone's laughter echoing from outside as the door shut harshly behind me. My heart dropped to my feet, and all my breath sucked out of my chest at once. It was so dark I couldn't see my hands in front of my face.

It only took a few seconds before the door burst back open and one of my friends pulled me out, wrapping me in a hug and apologizing, but I couldn't breathe.

It wasn't until a few minutes later, when I finally calmed down, that I realized that he was the only person close enough to push me into that room.

He'd pushed me in on purpose, only to be able to comfort me afterward, in some twisted attempt to win over my affection. After that, I could never think of him the same. From that moment on, I have always been very careful of who I open up to. I felt so betrayed, knowing that something so traumatic had been weaponized against me as some sort of joke. I tried to give my friend the benefit of the doubt. Had I only told him I was afraid of the dark, and not the reasons why? But I was close enough to this person that I was sure he knew.

Regardless whether my "friend" knew the severity of my fear or not, I don't believe someone who truly loves you would use you as the butt of a joke, unless they know you'd be able to laugh it off as well.

To me, that's the difference between fake friends and true friends. There are fake friends who will push you into the dark room, who will capitalize on your misery, and there are real friends who will stand by your side with a flashlight. There are fake friends who will try and talk you out of your pain, as if it's an inconvenience to them, and real friends who will want to listen and shoulder it with you, who will allow you to heal on your own time.

But sometimes the people closest to me are the ones actively rooting against me. Whether it be fair-weather friends who only want to be around when life is exciting, or friends who gossip behind my back and share my personal information with strangers, I've developed an extensive list of red flags to look out for.

This is when the second part of your question comes into play. *How do you even find real friends in the first place?* That's a hard one to answer. I've been forced to learn how to navigate cutting off bad friends, but for a while I didn't know how to welcome new people into my life in their place. We put a lot of emphasis on those red flags when it comes to friendships and relationships. But what about the green flags?

Try to think of it like this. Who do you feel the best version of yourself around? Who do you instantly want to go to with good news? Who do you know will defend your name even when you're not in the room? Who remembers the small details about you without being asked? I started looking for those people and keeping them close.

At the end of the day, it's our responsibility to look out for ourselves, and I have done so much growing on my own—but the people closest to me have been indispensable on that journey. They motivate me—without even trying—to live up to the person they see me as.

Everyone deserves a true friend. Even if it's only one person. I've always loved the saying "Four quarters are better than one hundred pennies." Apply this to your life and remember you are worthy of love and true friendship in the first place. You have to be your own best friend, too. It starts there.

Dear Madison,

Why music? What drew you to it in the first place? What about it makes you keep going when it gets hard?

Rydell, Georgia

It's not a coincidence my debut album was called *Life Support*. Music has been the only constant in my life for as long as I can remember. When I was seven, confused and dealing with the ramifications of my parents' divorce, I was drowning in music. It was not only my way of distracting myself; it was therapy. I was a smart kid, but I struggled in school, and the more I fell behind academically, the more I clung to music as my safe space, where I could find confidence. It gave me dreams and goals and things to work toward, when otherwise I would have been floating aimlessly without any sense of direction.

But as I grew older, my connection to music really took root and developed into something deeper. Discovering new music that put a voice to the way I was feeling was the only thing that made me feel less alone. In all the hours I spent locked away in my bedroom as a teenager, I was listening to music. In the constant change of scenery, music was there. I love old music the most. In my late teens, I did a deep dive into music from all different time periods, and I continue to draw inspiration from all eras. Something about that simplicity and nostalgia helps me escape when I need it most.

But the reason I do this extends outside just a collection of notes in a melody. Some of my favorite songs aren't even in English. I can't understand a word of them, and yet somehow they bring me so much comfort. In times when I can't begin to put how I'm feeling into words, music does it for me. There's no other experience like listening to a song—something you can do completely alone, yet feel so connected to the artist who wrote it. Something greater connects humankind to music, and I don't think there will ever be a way to describe it with language.

It took a while for me to find a team of people I felt fully comfortable making music with, and it took me even longer to build up my confidence in my own writing abilities. But once I did, it was like the world opened up before me. I become a different person when I'm in the studio. It's really the only time I can shut out everything else around me and focus on one thing. There's no better feeling than driving home from a studio session knowing I wrote a meaningful song, and feeling the weight of all those harbored emotions fall off my shoulders. I get to create something that's never existed before—a song that no one else but me could write—and put it out into the world. There's magic there, I'm sure of it. And I feel so blessed that this is what I get to do with my life. I can't imagine where I would be if that wasn't the case.

The hope of being able to help people with my music is why I went independent when I was dropped by my label; it's what gave me the courage to step forward into that scary unknown. It's why I persevere even when outside pressures wear on me. You could hand me a list of cons ten miles long, and it would still be worth it for me, even if the only thing I got to do was make music. It's always been the light at the end of the tunnel.

Long story short, you asked, "Why music?" and I'll tell you this: quite simply, music has always been there for me. It never turned a cold shoulder or left me alone. Contributing anything to such a universal gift as music is an honor.

I like to say I owe it to my teenage self to write the songs that she needed to hear. And I owe it to the little girl I once was, who belted out made-up songs without a care for how she sounded, just so I can tell her, "Yeah, you're going to go through some rough times, but you're going to create something so beautiful out of it, and that makes it all worth it in the end."

13

The Greener Grass

I touch on a lot of negatives in this book—enough that most of you have probably wondered why I wouldn't just give up and choose something different to do with my life, something less visible. At my worst, I've wondered the same thing. But then I look across my room and see a scrapbook of letters my fans put together for me, or I step onstage and see every individual face in the crowd before me, and everything gets put into perspective.

For a long time, I always said that making music and performing are what I was put on this earth to do, but I've come to realize that my purpose is even simpler than that—to connect with people. Music and performing are the avenues that get me there, but it's the moments of human connection they foster that make me feel like I've truly found what makes me me. It's why I wanted to write this book. It's why I created a special Q&A session before all of my shows, because there's nothing I love more than being able to sit down with my fans and talk about life, and offer my advice in any way that I can. It extends far beyond just the music.

I would go through it all over again, a million times over, if it meant gaining the audience I've gained. The love I have been shown is far warmer and kinder than any coldness of negativity. You hear people say it all the time, but I mean it with everything in me when I say my fans are the reason I do what I do. I hate to even call them fans. Some of them have been with me from the very beginning, and I consider them friends—we've watched each other grow up.

I value my connection with them over anything else. They allow me to be human, they listen to my scatterbrained stories and empathize with me, and in return I try my best to keep as close to them as possible. They've believed in me in times when I didn't believe in myself, and they've allowed me to grow and evolve without making me feel bad for changing or for trying out different things. When my debut album was pushed back over a year, they listened to apology after apology and still responded with the utmost excitement. When I started experimenting with different styles of music after I was dropped, they received it all with open arms, and their enthusiasm rubbed off on me.

It was actually then—when I first gained creative control over my music and started putting out songs that I'd written myself— that things shifted. Not only was writing lyrics a form of therapy for me, but getting to release those songs and hear feedback from my fans changed the way I viewed songwriting. I had fans before, sure, but they were fans of bubblegum pop songs that didn't carry much meaning for me. Now I can hear them quote specific lyrics I've written and tell me how much it helped them.

I didn't realize how impactful it would be for me. My music was helping my fans in the same way other artists had helped me through my roughest patches. I was connecting with people I'd never met, from all different walks of life, through lyrics I'd written during a time when I was terrified of being the only person feeling such intense emotions. Nothing else could do that. Nothing else could bring me that level of connection.

Writing a song about my own struggles and hearing it sung back to me is indescribable. A huge part of my love for music and songwriting is how music resonates so differently with each person who hears it. It's amazing to me how we can all enjoy a song for our own diverse reasons. It unifies us and brings us together.

On the recent tour for my album *Life Support*, I held meet and greets with about 150 people a night. I would chat and take a photo with each person, and then we had a short Q&A section before each show. Every person I met had a different story they wanted to share, or personal questions they could only ask one-on-one with me. I looked forward to it every night. This was where I got to really see where my music made its impact.

During one of those meet and greets, a teary-eyed fan told me how much my song "Homesick" meant to them—how it was the only song they'd listened to since their father passed away, and how it had helped them make it through. It's hard for me to wrap my head around something like that sometimes. I'm who someone turns to in such a hard and devastating time? Why me?

I was incredibly moved, but at first, I was confused when they mentioned "Homesick." It wasn't one of my more popular songs, and when I wrote it, it was about my own isolation—how I didn't feel I fit in on this planet and was homesick for a different world. But then they told me how hard the line "I wish you took me with you when you left that day" hit them after they lost their father.

I was struck by this. This song was not at all written about missing someone who has passed, yet this person made that connection. It was so touching and beautiful to me. I gave them a big hug and promised I would sing the song in their father's honor that night. Safe to say, we both cried.

By the middle of the tour, I heard similar stories over and over, that same line being interpreted that same exact way. I had been a comfort for people going through such serious loss, and I had no idea. I had no idea the reach that song had.

I am so honored to connect with people in this way. It is a gift that I will never take for granted, and knowing I can be there for them in times of need makes everything more than worth it. And those who listen to my music have gotten me through my own personal struggles just by lending me their ear. They've been there for me more than they'll ever know.

I mentioned how I feel like my role on this planet is changing. Sometimes I talk to friends about past relationships, how maybe someone you thought was meant to be your husband was actually in your life to teach you far greater lessons. I love thinking of things this way. Growing up, I have always told myself my life's purpose is to make music and to sing. But as I continue to grow and get older, I am learning it is so much more than that.

I recently spoke at a local high school in Los Angeles, coincidentally about a lot of topics I touch on in this book. About a year before, I ran into a few girls who attended the school in a Barnes & Noble, where they told me all about their club and asked if I would ever consider speaking to the members. I was beyond excited. When we finally got the event planned, I didn't show up pretending to be a mental health expert, but just as someone who had experiences that I hoped would help others by sharing.

After the event wrapped up, many of the students stayed behind to talk to me one-on-one. Everyone had a story to tell—a personal experience of mine they could relate to. Some asked for advice, some just wanted a hug.

One girl in particular sticks with me. She came up to me already teary-eyed, and the moment she started talking, all of her tears spilled forward. I pulled her away from the crowd so we could be alone, and she opened up about her breakup, confessing how she felt herself falling into a very deep depression. As she spoke, I was hit with a sudden impulse.

"Sorry if this is weird, but can I hold your hand?" I asked. Something came over me—I needed to show her she was loved.

"Of course you can," she answered, and now there we were—two strangers who had never met ten minutes before—standing in front of each other, crying and holding hands, with a new profound mutual understanding.

I think back to this moment often. What an honor I have been given in this life to have these experiences. There isn't a thing I would change. Somehow, years of negativity, hatred, depression, and (oftentimes) regret can be outshined and overshadowed by one fifteen-minute conversation, where I get to reach out my hand, share a story of mine, and connect with someone on such a human level.

I thank people like this girl for showing me why I'm still here. I thank people like this girl for showing me that while I did miss out on some teenage activities growing up, what I have gained in return is far more meaningful. I thank them for reminding me that I made the right choice—without a doubt—in sticking it out until this point.

14

"Drink Me"

Whenever I'm interviewed on a red carpet, people always comment on how much I touch my hair, or how I keep stealing glances at myself on the monitor—usually to try and paint me as vain and self-absorbed.

In reality, the times where I'm picking over myself the most, primping at my hair, checking to make sure my makeup looks okay, are when I'm the most insecure. Of course I'm going to make sure I look good on camera, because I know if I don't, it will be blown up and pointed out to me, over and over. It's the opposite of self-obsession. It's fear and insecurity.

We use a lot of similar words to describe women. If they're not self-obsessed, they're bitchy. If they're not bitchy, they're a diva. I could go on for days.

But what do all of these words have in common? They're all terms used strictly against women. To devalue them. When one of my male peers stands up for himself, he's called "headstrong" or "driven." But if I were to do the same, I'd risk being called "a bitch" or "stubborn."

It has happened to me enough times to be proven fact. I have a pretty strong will, and I'm very passionate about my work, but I've been deemed "difficult" for not wanting to bend on certain aspects of my vision. Simultaneously, I watch male artists be praised for being "rock stars" when they are five hours late to set.

For a long time, I shrank myself out of fear. I didn't want to be "too much." I had big ideas and big opinions, but the last thing I wanted was to be labeled a diva, or a bitch, or self-centered. After getting dropped from my label, I felt like I was walking on eggshells with every opportunity I was given, like one wrong move could sweep the rug out from under my feet all over again. Everyone around me told me it all could be taken away at any minute, and to me that meant *Smile, nod, shut up, and look pretty.*

I spent a lot of time silencing myself in rooms where decisions about my career were being made. I sat through songwriting sessions where male writers would overpower my creative decisions, even if it was for a song I'd conceptualized myself.

But as I've grown, I've stepped into myself, and learned how to pick my battles. I felt like Alice in Wonderland, chugging the "Drink Me" bottle and suddenly being thirty feet tall, growing into my voice and my power. I've learned to be unflinching when I have to be, how to speak up for myself when I need to, and how to walk out of rooms where I'm not being respected. It was all part of that promise I made to myself about staying alive. These were the things I needed to do to heal.

Part of finding my voice was simply through honing my talents outside of singing. I used to believe that singing was all I was good at—that all I had to do was show up, sing the lyrics, and let the experts handle the rest. But the more time I spent in the industry, the more I started picking up different talents and interests. I was a sponge, surrounded by creative people and eager to learn whatever I could. Who wouldn't be?

Now, I can't imagine leaving my career decisions up to anyone else. After my run as an independent artist, I fought to sign with a label that gave me creative control, and I don't take that for granted. When I was negotiating contracts, the conversation was no longer about my "image." The biggest thing I wanted was control. Everything I accomplished independently had skyrocketed my confidence. I proved to myself that I *could* manage my own career, and do it successfully.

I didn't need a label, and, walking into these meetings, I knew that. If they wanted me, it was about what they could offer to help me achieve *my* vision, not what I could do to live up to theirs.

Now, I'm a writer on every song of mine. I annoy my producers by hovering over their shoulders while they make edits and layer my vocals. I direct or codirect all my videos and intend to do so for the foreseeable future. When I planned my tour, I spent hours sitting on the studio floor with my choreographer and creative director, scouring over everything, down to the tiniest details—the shade of pink in the stage lighting, the number of seconds between songs, the placement of pearls on my costumes.

Sometimes being this involved means stepping on some toes.

When I was first trying to take charge, it was a fight to be taken seriously. I'd ask to sit in on editing meetings, or mixing sessions, and get looks from the experts, as if to say, *What do you know about this?* But I demanded that space be made for me. Especially when it came to my debut album and singles, it was *my* name that was on the line. I needed to ensure that what I was putting out was representing me to the best of my ability.

Fighting for myself and my vision has been an uphill battle. I've sat in rooms full of people who are all excited about a music video idea, ready to green-light it, and had to find the courage to disagree with them all. I've turned down prospective brand deals that would boost my career because I didn't want to promote a certain product to my impressionable audience. I've turned down video treatments that I felt were sexualizing me without any cause, even though that's what "sells" in our current climate. If I'm not comfortable, it's not happening.

But being in control comes with a lot of responsibility. And it means that when things don't go as planned, the blame falls on my shoulders. That's where my single "Selfish" comes in.

From the time my writers and I came up with the first lyrics, I knew this song was something special. It wasn't just a bouncy pop song I enjoyed dancing to. It was a personal, raw song, and my entire heart was in it. I knew in my gut that "Selfish" was my next single.

It just felt right. It was a connection point between me and my audience, showcased a new, more vulnerable side of me, and was a lyrical step up from anything I'd ever released before.

But those types of songs aren't usually released as singles. And the next song I released was going to be a pivotal moment in my career. The song would be one of the lead singles from my album, introducing me all over again after a long break from releasing music. And aside from that, I had to show my new label what I was capable of. There was so much riding on this moment.

Everyone else wanted me to release my other song, "Baby." On paper, coming out of the gates with that song was the smarter option. That was the typical formula—release a dancey summer pop song that gets stuck in your head and doesn't go away, and put out a fun, sexy music video that gets quick views. But as much as everyone on my team encouraged me to stick with the tried-and-true formula, we'd already done that before. I wanted "Selfish." And I refused to fold.

Running with "Selfish" as the next single meant convincing everyone, over and over, of what I already knew—that a confessional, vulnerable song was what I needed to connect with my audience. That my fans were smart enough to tell when I was being genuine in my music, that "Selfish" was a song that could help them with their own struggles.

Eventually I won the battle, but I knew I would only be proven right if the song performed well. It took a lot of faith in myself and my creative conviction to keep from taking the safe route—to keep from throwing my hands up and saying, "Okay, fine, let's just go with what works."

I had big visions for the music video (which I got to codirect), but because of budgeting issues we ended up settling on a simpler, pared-down version of what I wanted, which only put more pressure on the song alone. Without a flashy music video, the music needed to speak for itself. In hindsight, I'm glad that's the route we took, because it gave the song its moment to shine.

And shine it did. We released the song and music video on Valentine's Day 2020, and the response was immediate. It grew quickly, and today it remains my most successful song. Hearing all the positive feedback—from both the fans and the media—boosted my confidence immeasurably.

Over a year later, when the quarantine lifted in mid-2021, I finally performed "Selfish" in front of an audience for the first time. It'd been so long since the song was released that I thought I was used to performing it. I'd done several prefilmed performances, so I didn't think much of it when I showed up to perform it in person.

It didn't hit me until I stepped onstage and saw the audience in front of me. They sang every word along with me, and I cried my way through the entire song. Because of the pandemic, I'd only gotten to connect with them through a screen. I'd almost forgotten just how powerful live music is. I was reminded all over again why I love performing.

The positive response to "Selfish" ignited my confidence in myself and motivated me to continue following my gut when it came to my career. If the song hadn't performed well, I could have crawled back into my shell and let someone else take the lead. But now, because I'd been right about "Selfish," I'd proved that I knew my audience, and I knew what was right for my career. I wasn't going to let my voice be doubted anymore.

But I still encounter a lot of tests. My single "Reckless" was another song that I knew was a single from the moment it was born. It was another step in the direction of solidifying my sound, and as I started brainstorming the music video, I quickly realized it was going to be a big undertaking.

I wanted a car. I wanted a giant custom music box. I wanted the best slow-motion camera we could get. I wanted rigged stunts, an underwater scene, and custom costumes. The vision was so clear in my head that I couldn't imagine sacrificing anything to make it easier. But translating it onto paper was difficult, and when I presented the idea to my team, it took a lot of convincing to make them see the same vision I did.

I went in strong. I told them exactly what I needed and made it clear that the decision was made. When they questioned me, I was prepared. But after some debate, I could tell the mood was still hesitant.

"It's happening," I told them. "It's happening, and it's going to happen the way I want it to. So you can either get behind it, or I'll front the rest of the money myself." (Which is what ended up happening.)

Later that day, I was out at the mall when my phone buzzed in my pocket. The name on the screen made me tense. I love my managers, but usually I only get those kind of unprompted calls when there is some sort of problem. I knew I'd been a bit forthright in the meeting before, and I grew scared it had done the opposite of what I wanted.

"Hello?" I picked up, stepping outside the store.

"Hey, Madison."

"Hey." I laughed under my breath. "I have a feeling I already know what this is about . . ."

"Do you?" she asked, and I paused. I couldn't tell if she was being sarcastic or not.

"About what happened in that meeting?"

"Yeah. I heard about that," she said, and I waited for the inevitable. But then she laughed. "I'm pretty proud of you, Madison."

"Wait, what?"

"Okay, like, obviously maybe we can keep it to a calm discussion next time, but . . ."

I held my breath.

"But standing up for yourself like that took guts."

"I thought you were calling me to chew me out," I admitted, fiddling with the drawstring of my sweatpants as I watched people pass by.

"You have big opinions. That means you have a big vision. It's a good thing to know what you want," she said. "It's commendable."

"But they seemed pretty . . ." I paused, trying to find the right word. "Surprised? Unhappy?"

She laughed. "So what? Sure, you hurt a few egos. But think about it. Standing up for yourself means you care. You care enough about your work and your music that that passion spills over. You're only outspoken because you want it to perform to its full potential. That's how I've always seen it."

It'd been a long time since I felt that understood. Sometimes it seemed like I was fighting a never-ending battle when it came to my vision for my career.

"You've been in this for how many years, Madison?" she asked me.

"Ten."

"*Ten years* of experience," she emphasized. "You know what you're doing. It's not their career. It's not their name that has to take the fall if something goes wrong. I'd be more concerned if you sat in that room and let them make all the decisions for you. I would think you couldn't care less either way."

I sat with myself for a while after that call. For so long I'd let other people's doubts and opinions shrink me. I felt like I was swimming upstream to be taken seriously—like no matter how many times I proved myself capable, my judgment was still questioned. But as I've gotten older, my attitude has shifted. I've started welcoming the chance to prove people wrong.

Instead of trying to succeed out of spite, to stick it to the people who doubt me, I flip the narrative. "I will succeed to show the kids who look up to me that it's possible," I tell myself. I will succeed to forge a path for those who follow me.

At the end of the day, there are certain things I can't control. The only thing I'm in complete control of is myself, my actions, and my attitude. I could spend all the time in the world being upset at the circumstances, or mad at the industry as a whole for the way it sometimes works against artists, but that will only take me so far. I have to use that anger and frustration as fuel to do better, or it will only burn me into the ground. If I risk being called a diva just for standing up for myself, then it's a label I'll wear proudly.

Turning Negatives into Positives

All my life I've been labeled "overly sensitive," but I've always looked at my sensitivity as a sign of a big heart. What's so wrong about caring deeply?

Think about your own life. Name a trait that other people find "negative" about you.

Now find a way to turn it into a positive. Do you get called "stubborn" when you really just have strong opinions? Do you get called "picky" when you're really just detail-oriented? "Quiet" when you're simply better at expressing yourself on paper?

How did your parents handle you starting a career so young? Has your career ever gotten in the way of those relationships?

Piper, Maryland

My close relationship with my family keeps me grounded, but it took us a long time to get here. It was rocky at first. Moving to LA really split my family in two. My parents had been divorced for years by that point, but I grew up dividing my time between their houses, only a five-minute drive apart. Now, we were on different coasts. My mom gave up her own business to let me chase my dreams, my dad supported us from afar, and my brother was thrown into a new world. It was so much change so fast.

My mom was our rock through all the madness. She's my hero—present in every story I tell in this book, right behind me, pushing me to go on. I've learned so much from her just by watching the way she navigates the world.

As a child, I only saw my mother as strong and fearless. But now, I use different words to describe her. Not because she isn't strong and fearless, but because she is so much more. Now that I'm an adult, I've gotten to see the more vulnerable side of her. She no longer has to shield her little girl from the truth. She has broken down in front of me, and she has softened many times, which has only made me look at her with so much more admiration. I've learned a lot of the struggles she kept hidden from me—the silent battles she was fighting while trying to keep me together, too. She has shown me that life can be tough on you. Every day is not filled with sunshine, to say the least, and that is okay. But despite it all, she shoulders everything with such grace, and even on her worst days she treats every person with the utmost kindness.

During the pandemic, I came back to stay in New York with her for a few months, and it gave us a lot of time to reflect. I opened up to her about more of what I'd been through—some of the things I'd kept a secret from her at the time. One night she came in my room and sat on the edge of my bed, looked at me for a long while, and then shook her head.

"Did we do the right thing?"

"What?" I had no clue what she was talking about.

"Everything. Letting you move out to LA so young. Letting you get signed. Did I fuck up?" she asked. "Did I fuck *you* up?"

It's not that I ever blamed her. If she hadn't let me go for it, I think I would have spent the rest of my life resenting her for holding me back. I would have never stopped wondering, What if? How is a mother supposed to tell her child that they can't take a stab at a dream they've had for as long as they can remember?

"I didn't know it was like that," she continued. "I didn't know you felt like you'd lost your entire childhood. I thought it was what you wanted to do."

"It was what I wanted to do," I finally said, my voice softening as I thought it over. "I guess I just didn't understand how much I was giving up in the process."

Her face fell, but I shook my head. "It is what it is. You had no way of knowing, Mom. You did everything right."

If I'm being completely honest, I have a lot of guilt surrounding my brother, Ryder. He was around nine years old at the time I uploaded my YouTube video, and his life was uprooted just as much as mine was when I was first signed. I wasn't the only one pulled out of school—he was, too—and his entire life changed at the will of his sister's dreams, all completely out of his control. In those years, my career and my struggles sometimes overshadowed his. Coming to LA with my mom and me, he lost out on a lot of quality time with our dad and his hometown friends. He was always the shyer one, and just by being associated with me he was sometimes pulled into a spotlight that he didn't necessarily want to be in. I wouldn't blame him if he resents me for it all, because I know I'd feel slighted if I was in his shoes.

But my brother is also my rock. Not just because we're related by blood, but because he's one of the few people who knew me through it all. No one makes me laugh harder. We share a love and passion for music. When he came to my concert, he sobbed in my mom's arms. Somehow, in the face of an upbringing that could have turned him bitter and resentful, he is full of love, and he has done a remarkable job with the cards he was dealt. I am so proud of him.

My relationship with my dad is a little different. He raised a wildly independent, high-spirited daughter, and we butt heads a lot—probably because we're more similar than we are different. But as I've grown older, we've gotten closer. He's always the first to find the opportunity to brag about me, or push me when I need it the most, and it's in those moments I know in my heart how proud he is of me. You can catch him at my shows wiping a tear off his face and being the first to give me a hug as I step offstage. He has supported me every step of the way, even if that meant not seeing his children for weeks at a time. He has always been my number-one fan at his core, and he was the first person to truly believe in me. For my entire life, all I've ever wanted to do is make him proud.

When we're young, we don't really understand that our parents are human, too. And I spent most of my life thinking my mom and dad had it all figured out. But looking back, I can't imagine how scary it must have been for them when I first started this journey. My mom sacrificed everything for me—moving across the country on her own and navigating an industry she knew nothing about. And both of my parents lost sleep every night, wondering if they were doing what was best for their two children. It's only as I've gotten older that I've realized how much of a toll it must've taken on them, too.

I don't think we would be as close as we are if we hadn't gone through all of this together. I'm forever grateful for them.

Dear Madison,

I feel like a failure. Like I'm stuck in one place and everyone else around me is moving forward with their lives. I look at all my friends and it's like everything comes to them easily, but for me, I have to fight just to get out of bed in the morning.

The more time passes, the more it feels like I'll never catch up.

I don't know what I want. Where do I even begin?

Aaron, California

Start by being gentle with yourself.

We put a lot of pressure on ourselves to reach certain milestones by certain markers. We compare ourselves to our friends and put ourselves in silent competition with the people around us. *I need to have everything planned out by the time I turn eighteen,* we tell ourselves. *If I don't have my dream job by twenty-five, I never will. If I'm not making this much money by thirty, I'm a failure.*

But we don't see the entirety of our friends' lives. They could be struggling just as much as you and just putting on a brave face. And if you're comparing your life to the lives of people you follow on social media, not many people are honest about the hard things. Everyone's putting their best foot forward online. We post about the colleges we get into, but not the ones we get rejected from. We post pictures at weddings, but rarely at funerals. You're only seeing a small percentage of everyone's lives.

To start, if you're happy where you are—if you only feel pressured to change because everyone else around you is doing it—your motivation won't last. Your desire to change has to come from inside yourself.

But if your unhappiness feels like restlessness, if *you* want to grow and you don't know how, that's a healthy place to start.

Life isn't a competition. It's not a race that needs to be won. There is no end goal. No time limit. Everyone has different starting points and different obstacles they have to overcome.

But at the same time, everyone has different goals and desires—that's the beauty of it. Some people want a quiet life, some want a loud life. Some people want big, demanding careers, and some don't. Some people find their dream jobs at twenty, and some people don't know what they want to do until they're in their fifties. There's no step-by-step guide or formula to life. Sure, it can be intimidating, but it's also comforting that no matter what you choose to do with your time on this planet, as long as you're not hurting anyone, there's no wrong choice. You set your own definition of success.

Personally, my journey has taught me that sometimes I can't force myself to grow. A lot of healing comes naturally, and it can't be rushed.

Sometimes we just need time. And patience with ourselves.

Sometimes, without reason or formula, we evolve.

For years I tried crash diets and gimmicky health trends and only ended up hungry and miserable. But lately, I've been learning how to cook and trying new recipes, and for the first time, it's been an enjoyable process. I never saw it coming, I just woke up one day and decided I wanted to make a fancy dinner for myself, and it's grown slowly since then—even though I tried for years to force myself into the same mindset. Now, it's happened organically.

You can't hate yourself into the person you want to become. You can't hate your body into looking a different way. You can't hold yourself to an unrealistic standard and then punish yourself for falling short. Hating and criticizing yourself is backward progress.

At my lowest points, where I hated myself so much I didn't find myself worthy of that care, I started trying to step outside of myself.

If I made a mistake that I thought was irredeemable, I'd ask myself: If my best friend did this, would I judge her? Would I love her less? The answer was always no.

When I was in a relationship that made me feel bad about myself, I'd ask myself: If I saw my future daughter in this situation, what would I tell her to do? The answer was usually, Put yourself first.

You need to extend the same care, patience, and understanding to yourself as you do to the people around you. You have to start by treating yourself like a human.

For me, the driving force behind everything I do is following what feels genuine to me.

The common denominator of a lot of my lowest points was

that I put myself in situations—rooms of people, relationships, career choices—that didn't feel authentic to me.

We live in a world that tries to detach us from our bodies. I spent those miserable years ignoring my gut feelings and my intuition and trying to talk myself out of the way I felt. If I was introduced to a new person and immediately felt like something was off, I'd tell myself I was being dramatic and push it aside. But time after time, my initial instinct about them was proven right, and I only ended up wasting time on people who were rooting against my best interests.

In my journey, I've naturally fallen back in tune with my body—working with my intuition instead of against it. I've started listening to those gut feelings when something feels wrong. And when things feel right, when I get that strong, assured feeling deep in my heart, I pursue it. Sometimes our body knows what the mind hasn't figured out yet. Sometimes it's as easy as avoiding the bad feelings and following the happy feelings.

The rest followed naturally. I shifted my goals from physical, tangible achievements—numbers, timelines, awards—and started focusing on operating out of a place of authenticity.

I have things I want to achieve, sure. I have big plans for my career. I want to sell out Madison Square Garden someday. I want to continue to write songs that make an impact on people's lives.

But I also have goals in my personal life. I want to be a mother one day and build a family of my own. I want to go back to school and get a degree in psychology so I can use that education and my platform for good.

But I don't want any of those things if I have to betray myself to get them. I've realized that those achievements will only ever feel whole and fulfilling if the route I take to get there is genuine and fueled by the things that matter to me.

At the end of the day, I don't want to hurt other people to get what I want. I don't want to sell myself, or pretend to be someone I'm not, to appeal to a certain audience. I don't want to put myself in a position where I'm miserable and suffering mentally in order to push myself toward those goals.

If I get a Grammy for an album full of songs that aren't truthful to me, I don't want it. If I sell out Madison Square Garden because I'm singing songs I'm not proud of, I don't want it. I don't want to look back at my life and career once it's all said and done and feel like I had to be someone else to cheat my way to the top. When all the glitz and glamour are gone, I still have to go to bed with myself every night. I want to be able to sleep soundly, knowing I'm doing myself justice.

And it's my smaller goals that are going to help me take the steps to get there. My day-to-day decisions—taking care of my body and my mental health, and being intentional about who I keep in my close circle—are the driving forces behind all of the bigger, flashier accomplishments.

I take time to check in with myself and acknowledge the ways I've grown, no matter how small. To say, "Wow, this time last year, I would have handled this in a much unhealthier way." I'm still so young, and I have so many more years left to learn, and even though I don't exactly know who I am yet, I feel myself getting closer and closer to her every day. And more importantly, I'm enjoying the process.

It will happen for you, too. I promise. Be gentle with yourself on the way there.

Reconnecting with Yourself

I feel happiest when I'm _____.

When I'm complimented on my _____, I feel most seen.

I've always had a natural talent for _____

Even if I'm not the best at it, I still love to _____

My dream home is full of _____

In ten years, I want to be _____

The best gift I ever received was _____

15

Everything Happens for a Reason

One of my mom's favorite videos of me is from my kindergarten graduation. I'm waiting to sing the national anthem, holding a microphone bigger than my head as my teacher introduces me to the audience. "Remember the name Madison Beer," she says. "She's gonna make it. She's got real star potential."

For my mom, it's proof that her daughter was meant to perform; she's very proud of it. But for me, there's something bittersweet about it. Whenever it shows up on my timeline, I scroll past it.

It's hard for me to look at that little girl and know she had no idea what was to come—the good and the bad. At some of my lowest points, I avoided looking at old videos and photos altogether. They reminded me of an innocence I could never get back. I saw a little girl who felt like such a stranger to me. And I felt guilty. Guilty for some of the decisions I made that had hurt her, guilty for forgetting about her, guilty for not living up to all the big dreams she had for me.

One of the questions I get asked most in interviews is, "If you could say something to your younger self, what would it be?" For a long time I hated that question. There was so much I wanted to change—so many things I wished I could have done better, so many times I wanted to go back, grab my younger self by the shoulders, and steer her in a different direction. I would have given her a map of her life—the path of least resistance—and told her, "Follow this; this is how you avoid all the hurt."

But now I'm twenty-three years old, and I answer the question differently.

Now, it's scary for me to even think about going back and changing anything I've done, even my mistakes, because of the butterfly effect it could have on the rest of my future. I wouldn't choose to steer myself around the pain. Because I've had time to grow and gain distance, it's easier for me to put things in perspective. Now, when asked what I would tell my younger self, the answer that usually follows is: I would tell her I love her, and I would give her a huge hug.

For a long time I didn't do well with uncertainty. I wanted everything to have some sort of underlying lesson—like life was one big puzzle that I needed to unlock, like I could crack myself open like a fortune cookie and boil the meaning of life down to one single sentence. I don't know if I'll ever find it, but I've started making my own meaning out of things. Even if it's not true, I tell myself that the universe is always working in my best interests— that it shapes itself around the decisions I make, not the other way around. Just holding that mindset alone has helped me navigate the world.

I used to look at my sensitivity as a weakness. I wondered why I had to care so much, about everything, all the time. But now it is my true superpower. I am grateful to have a sensitive heart. I am lucky to love deeply. I know this now. My ability to be vulnerable with myself and others is strength, and nothing less.

I have to tell myself that the pain I went through was for a bigger purpose, because I don't want to live in a world where we suffer just to suffer. And even if that is true, I still refuse to let it be pointless. I make meaning out of it for myself—I try to turn my past suffering into something that can help me push forward and help those around me. Even if we can't make sense of it, life is inherently a gift, and I want to take full advantage of my time here.

I try to look at the world with the hope that, however cliché it sounds, everything really does happen for a reason.

Just recently, on the music video shoot for my single "Reckless," the last scene of the night was set to be shot in a water tank. It was late at night, and everyone—me, the crew, my team—was exhausted and ready to get the shot over with so we could go home. I was just stepping into the outfit for the final scene when one of my managers slipped into the room, an odd look on her face. She called me outside to talk, and I watched as all the production assistants scrambled around. I knew right away something was wrong.

The water tank I was supposed to shoot in had burst, and all the heated water spilled out, flooding the entire parking lot. There was no way it could be fixed on such short notice, but it was our last day of shooting this music video and it was a shot we *needed*—the pivotal scene that the entire music video leads up to. Even if we were able to get it fixed the following day, we didn't have the money for it. Underwater scenes are costly. And it would mean paying for another day with the slow-motion camera we were renting, along with another day's salary for the production crew and everyone else involved. I was funding most of the music video by myself. It just wasn't possible.

I'll admit, I cried. It was the last scene of a three-day shoot—for a music video I had written, starred in, *and* codirected. There was so much riding on the success of this video, and this happening at the last minute felt like a cruel joke. I was running on little to no sleep, and the only thing getting me through the day had been the knowledge that I'd be able to go home, get into bed, and sleep for as long as I wanted. Now, that wasn't the case.

But I didn't have long to wallow in self-pity. There was an entire crew waiting on my direction, and the only thing I could do was suck it up and figure out a solution. Wiping my eyes, I sat and brainstormed with the crew.

"We could drive two hours away, we could get there at midnight, wrap at four in the morning, and do this at a stage with a set tank," said one of the production managers.

"Who knows if we'd even be able to get in contact on such short notice," another person from the stunt department added. "We could call around and try to find another truck, but that might take—"

"I have a pool at my house . . ." I'd finally worked up the courage to say what I'd been thinking the entire time, fighting past my fear of sounding stupid after a half hour of debating. "I mean, that's close enough to a water tank, right?"

They all looked at each other before shrugging. "How far away do you live?"

Somehow, everyone working on the shoot chose to work overtime, packing up all the cameras, all the rigs we'd need, and lugging them all the way across town to my house. We all crammed into my backyard and buckled down, wasting no time in outfitting my pool and getting the final shot we needed—me diving into the water and then floating, suspended and motionless, for about thirty seconds.

I had to dive headfirst into my pool over and over until it was perfect. And then another shot that required holding my breath and keeping entirely still, even though the water was trying to pull me to the surface. I don't know how I managed it. Every time they called cut, I'd reemerge from the water to catch my breath, and all the water that I inhaled flooded out of my nose and mouth. It felt like there was pool water in my brain. I couldn't help but laugh.

By the time we wrapped, it was five in the morning. I was freezing cold, dripping wet, and struggling not to fall asleep standing up, but the smile on my face was genuine. We all huddled around the small monitor to watch the takes we'd gotten. It looked even better than I'd imagined. It was perfect.

"Wait, these are insane," I said, my teeth chattering. "Would we have been able to get shots like these in that small tank? Why didn't we think of using my pool in the first place?"

Amber, my codirector, laughed and shook her head. "You remember how small that water tank was? This is ten times better than anything we could have built on set."

I wrapped my towel tight around myself and hung back as the rest of the crew started packing up.

"You know, you're pretty lucky that tank broke when it did," one of the men spoke up. "The lining was plastic, and it ripped from the bottom, so all the water got sucked through like a funnel. If you had already been in the water, you would have been dragged under, too. With all the wood supports, you could've gotten badly injured. Or stuck underwater."

I shivered. I was ready to walk out of the dressing room when the tank burst. It was a matter of minutes before I would have gotten into the water.

"So be glad it happened when it did," he added, laughing. "You got lucky."

Looking back, I can't even imagine what the shots would have looked like if we hadn't gotten them in my pool. At the time—at the end of a grueling shoot day—hearing that the water tank had burst felt like the end of the world. But not only did it save me from potentially getting seriously injured, shooting in my pool ended up working out better in the end.

I'll never know exactly why it happened, but I went to bed that night feeling oddly grateful that it had.

When I look back on everything I've gone through, I feel the same way. There have been so many moments where I've been mad at the world, when I've been terrified of my future. Sometimes I wish I could go back and tell that girl, "You have nothing to be afraid of, just ride it out, I promise it will all make sense in the end." I try to remind myself of the same when I'm struggling— that there's a version of me in the future that is waiting for me, grateful for the lessons that I'm being taught presently, even if right now they feel pointless.

Having my nudes leaked felt unnecessarily cruel and painful, but years later I was able to use my experience to speak out publicly and help other young women going through similar trauma.

Being sexually assaulted at fourteen at my first Los Angeles party is still something I can't make sense of, but it has made me an advocate for sexual assault victims, and it is not something I am ashamed of. I am proud that I get to relate to others who have had similar experiences. I find strength in that.

Getting dropped by my first label felt like the end of my career, but really it was just the push I needed to find myself artistically.

Cutting off toxic friends and partners was painful, but it opened up a place in my life for new, beautiful connections to blossom.

If I hadn't tried to take my own life, I wouldn't have made my crossroads decision the following day, and I wouldn't have taken the steps to recovery.

I've known real, deep pain, but my journey to healing has given me tools that I can extend outside myself, and allowed me to be a role model to anyone who'd like to listen.

And everything I've gone through has allowed me to write this book, put it in your hands, and hopefully make a few of you feel less alone.

I have to believe everything happens for a reason, because it hasn't let me down so far, and it has all led me to you. I might not know you, but I see you and am thanking you and holding you through these words. Thank you for doing the same for me.

I only hope to leave you feeling like you know me a little bit better, for whatever it's worth. I hope you see this as an example that we are all just human beings trying our best with the cards we've been dealt. I hope it prompts you to be a little softer, a little kinder, to both yourself and the people around you.

And finally, now that you know some chapters of my life, I hope you're reminded that everyone has a story that you just haven't read yet. Thank you for reading some of mine.

With love,
Madison

Acknowledgments

THANK YOU.

Tracie Beer, the best mother I could ever ask for. I am lucky to be your daughter.

Robert Beer, my biggest fan from day one. I wouldn't be me without you. The first person to believe in me.

Ryder Beer, your strength and resilience have moved and touched me in ways I am unsure you will ever understand. Thank you for bearing the hard times with grace. Being your sister has been life's greatest gift.

Lena Fultz, you showed me what true friendship is. You are so important to me, and I will forever be so honored and grateful to know you and to be able to call you my best friend. Thank you for giving me the bravery and strength to talk about these things. I love you more than words. Thank you for being a guiding light in the dark. You're my hero.

Prescilla Lovett, essentially my second mother. Pres, my memories of you singing to me in the bath as a child will never leave me. Thank you for being one of the most impactful people I have ever known. I love to sing because of you. I love you.

Leroy Clampitt, I feel lucky to know you. A generational talent whom I somehow got lucky enough to collaborate with on, well, everything. Thank you for always going with me, never against me. Thank you for pushing me to be better and more every single time. Your friendship and spirit have inspired me and changed me. I love you, kiwi.

Jeremy Dussolliet and Tim Sommers (Kinetics & One Love), two boys whom I love more than anything. The instant connection I felt with you both was unlike any other. There is so much I can say. I feel like I have known you for a lifetime, and our friendship means so much to me. I am so proud of you both and so eternally grateful you have blessed my music with your contributions and talents. I hope you guys know there is no one I would rather make music with for the rest of my life than you. K-1L forever.

Nick Cullen, my homeschool teacher from ninth to twelfth grade, who was truly the first person to make me feel like I had a voice that should be heard. Thank you for making me feel like I had intelligence that shouldn't be ignored. Your support in those years changed me forever. You are remarkable.

Oscar Scivier, the person who single-handedly restored my faith in the industry. We have been through so much together, and I will cherish our memories for a lifetime. Thank you for everything.

Sarah Stennant, thank you for believing in me and picking me up off my feet when it felt like no one else would. I look up to you in so many ways.

About the Author

After going viral at just twelve years old, MADISON BEER publicly navigated the transition from childhood star to global entertainer, undergoing a record-breaking run as an independent artist before signing with Epic Records and releasing her long-awaited debut album, *Life Support*, in 2021. Known for her vulnerability and authenticity both inside and outside of the music industry, Beer has built her platform on speaking openly about her experiences with being in the public eye at such a young age. Through sharing the highs and lows of her journey, Beer resonates deeply with an audience that looks to her as more of a friend than as an untouchable celebrity.

Beer is now the master of her own creative domain, from inception to realization, including writing and producing her own music to conceptualizing and directing her music videos. In addition to her art, Beer also provides her work as a mental health advocate and philanthropist, with hopes of returning to school to study psychology. She currently resides in Los Angeles.